Trams and Trolleybuses in Doncaster

TRAMS AND TROLLEYBUSES
in Doncaster

Richard Buckley

Wharncliffe Books

First Published in 2003 by
Wharncliffe Books
an imprint of
Pen and Sword Books Limited,
47 Church Street, Barnsley,
South Yorkshire. S70 2AS

Copyright © Richard Buckley 2003

For up-to-date information on other titles produced under the
Wharncliffe imprint, please telephone or write to:

> **Wharncliffe Books**
> **FREEPOST**
> **47 Church Street**
> **Barnsley**
> **South Yorkshire S70 2BR**
> **Telephone (24 hours): 01226 - 734555**

ISBN: 1-903425-29-8

A CIP catalogue record of this book is available from the
British Library

Front Cover illustration: *Silver Street from Cleveland Street, Doncaster*

Printed in the United Kingdom by
CPI UK

PREFACE

This volume finds its origin from the happy conjunction of a lifelong interest in tramways, a period of residence in Doncaster and the need to find a subject for some academic research. The book in its present form could not have been written, however, without the willing cooperation of many people more knowledgeable than I am, especially when it comes to trolleybuses. Stanley Frith, Harold Green, Mrs R Roberts, Miss J Thorne and Geoff Warnes brought history to life through their personal reminiscences. Rosie Thacker provided her usual helpful support at the National Tramway Museum. I am grateful to the following for permission to use their own photographs or for the loan of material in their possession: Rod Bramley, David Clarke, Dancerama, The Reverend Michael Faulkner, Dennis Gill, Charles Hall, Mary House, David Packer, R Priestley, Mrs R Roberts, Lyndon Rowe, Howard Turner and Geoff Warnes. Various interesting views were obtained from the Old Barnsley stall of Barnsley market which, despite its name, stocks a wide variety of South Yorkshire material. Roger Smith drew the maps with his usual accuracy and clarity. A full history of Doncaster Corporation Transport remains to be written, but I hope that this book will reveal at least a handful of new facts and that the illustrations will bring back memories of the times and streets through which the vehicles ran.

INTRODUCTION

Doncaster was founded to serve the requirements of transport when the Romans built a small fort at their military road crossing of the River Don in the First Century AD. Much later, medieval pilgrims might have paused to pray at the chapel on St Mary's Bridge, whilst passengers during the coaching era certainly did break their journeys at some of the inns along the Great North Road. By 1835 fourteen London-bound coaches were stopping daily. The river and canals had grown in importance during the eighteenth century, as did horse racing, if that can be called transport. The railway certainly may, however, and in 1850 the London to York main line was completed. In 1853 the Great Northern Railway sited its workshops in Hexthorpe, and that single step transformed Doncaster into an industrial town almost overnight. Over 6,000 men came to be employed at the Plant, as it was known. The town's population grew accordingly, from 5,697 in 1801, to 12,052 in 1851 and, by the last census of the century, to nearly 26,000. A lot of other places, like Balby, were then outside the Borough, so the overall population was much greater (it was 59,890 in 1929, and even then Bentley and Woodlands were both still separate). Urban transport was becoming a necessity. But how was it to be provided?

As far back as the year 1800 sedan chair carriers had plied their trade, taking fashionable inhabitants and their guests to receptions at the Mansion House (built in 1744-50 and one of only three in the country). But in an industrial age, it was the common person who required transport to work and to the shops. The first horse bus services were started in 1887 by J G Steadman, a local undertaker (John Heath of Sheffield took a similar step at about the same time). He was joined in 1889 by Hodgson & Hepworth, a firm of grocers in St Sepulchre Gate, who saw the potential for delivering customers to their door. The third operator was J Stoppani and, sometimes in competition, they ran buses to Avenue Road, Balby, Bentley, Hexthorpe, Hyde Park and the Racecourse. Well before this, in 1878, proposals had been made for a tramway (almost certainly also horse powered), but nothing came of that, nor of an 1895 scheme for a line to Balby.

In 1898, however, the British Electric Traction Company (BET) drew up plans for routes to Avenue Road, Balby, Bentley and Hexthorpe and took the first steps towards applying for legal sanction for them. The BET was definitely big business and was known by its opponents as 'the Octopus'; public authorities were usually highly suspicious of it and its motives. This was the heyday of municipal socialism and municipalities preferred wherever possible to own and operate their own services. Doncaster Council had already decided to build an electric power station and a tramway would be an ideal customer. So they presented their own proposals and the BET withdrew, though not without first offering to lease the completed lines. The Council system was not dissimilar, but had additional branches to Hyde Park and the Racecourse. Most tramways were authorised under the 1870 *Tramways Act* and Doncaster may have been the first Council to make use of the 1896 *Light Railways Act* instead, which had certain advantages to the promoters. A hearing was held at the Mansion House in February 1899 and, in marked contrast to modern planning enquiries, took only one day. The only serious objection came from the railway companies, who did not want trams crossing their main line between London and Edinburgh. Lord Jersey, the President of the Light Railway Commissioners, agreed with them, so the Order was granted subject to the planned route to Bentley being detached, pending the construction of a bridge. The whole tramway scheme was expected to cost £70,000.

There was a delay of two years before construction began. Pointwork was supplied by Hadfields of Sheffield, but the track itself came from Belgium. Cravens, the wagon builders of Darnall, had tendered for the car bodies, but the contract went to a firm who could supply complete trams (full details of the trams are given in the fleet list at the end of this book, as well as in the photos and captions). There were to be fifteen of them, which makes the decision to build three depots appear somewhat prodigal. An extra one in Marsh Gate on the Bentley side of the railway was essential, but two were planned in the town, one in Greyfriars Road and the other in part of the Wool Market; the latter idea was quickly abandoned, however. The rail itself was non-standard as it had a groove in the centre (it was usually along the inner edge), but much more serious was the fact that the foundations were skimped for reasons of economy. In later years the track was continually being repaired. A further mistake, though more forgivable, was that the loans for construction were taken out over a forty year period; experience quickly showed that even well laid tramway track would be life-expired well within that time scale. The Council had hoped to spread the repayments over sixty years.

The first two routes, to Balby and Hexthorpe, were opened on 2 June 1902 and by January 1903 all the originally proposed system was up and running. Further Light Railway Orders were obtained in

1902, 1903, 1911 and 1914; the lines across the North Bridge were laid as part of the powers for the bridge, obtained in 1908. The first two Orders largely provided for various deviations and additions to the existing or planned routes, but the second also authorised two completely new branches, one to Beckett Road and the other through Oxford Street. The 1911 Order was for two extensions, from Bentley to New Bentley and from Balby to Warmsworth, and, finally, a complete branch was authorised to Brodsworth; all these were a response to the growth of a new industry around Doncaster as the concealed coalfield was exploited by new deep mines, to each of which a rapidly growing pit community became attached. A contemporary brochure said that the development had happened 'almost by the stroke of a magician's wand'. By 1911 Brodsworth and Bentley pits together employed about 2,000 men and boys. The opening and closing dates for all the tram routes are given in Table 1.

Table 1
TRAMWAY ROUTES

Route	Opened	Extended	Closed
Balby	2 Jun 1902	★★	25 Jul 1931
Hexthorpe	2 Jun 1902	–	30 Jun 1929
Racecourse	30 Jun 1902	1903	15 Jan 1930
Hyde Park	1 Aug 1902	Oct 1902	15 Jan 1930
Bentley	27 Oct 1902	20 Mar 1913	21 Aug 1928
Avenue Rd	15 Jan 1903	–	mid-1920s
Beckett Rd	17 Aug 1903	–	30 Jul 1929
Oxford St	25 Nov 1903	–	18 May 1907
Warmsworth★★	4 Feb 1915	Late 1919	25 Jul 1931
Brodsworth	21 Feb 1916	–	8 Jun 1935

The Hyde Park route was to have finished at the end of Catherine Street, but in 1902 it was decided to continue it along Carr House Road as far as Jarrett Street; this extension opened only two months after the initial section. Of the two entirely new lines, that to Beckett Road was uncontentious, though most of it lay outside the Borough. The boundaries were extended in 1914 and again in 1936, by which time the authority had become a County Borough (in 1927). The shorter route, to Oxford Street, was included because of pressure from local councillors and residents. When it was being planned a property owner in the area wrote to the Board of Trade (or BOT, the

Government Department responsible for tramways) that 'the line is entirely unwanted. From any point along the route a tram line can be reached within a quarter of a mile'. This assessment was unfortunately quite correct. Between 7 December 1903 and 2 January 1904 only 3,633 passengers were carried at a fare of 1d (less than $^1/_2$ p) giving total receipts of about £15, whereas the Balby trams had earned £187 from over 46,000 passengers in the same period. By March trams were run only after 1 pm. And in May it was agreed to restrict the service to Friday and Saturday evenings. Unsurprisingly, it ceased to be worthwhile running any trams, and the service seems to have stopped entirely by July 1905. In April 1907 the Tramways' Committee (actually the Electricity and Tramways' Committee) decided to have another try, this time at the reduced fare of $^1/_2$ d, but once again few passengers were attracted and the line closed for ever on 18 May. Over ambitious expansion was not confined to Doncaster or indeed to the UK. Many tramways had one or more non-paying routes, though it was the smaller undertakings who were more likely to give up and close them, for obvious reasons. For example, a branch of the Stassenbahn Herne – Castrop-Rauxel in Germany was closed after less than four years and a later experiment with one-man trams lasted little more than a year before final closure.

Of the original lines, that to the Racecourse was the most interesting. At this period many tens of thousands of racegoers used public transport to reach the course, which was quite a long way beyond the built-up area. The 1899 powers envisaged the usual economical single and loop tramway, but it was realised before it opened that this was insufficient. Track doubling could be agreed by the BOT without the need for parliamentary approval, and it was, but the 1902 Order was used to gain permission for a siding off the main road alongside the stands. However, the bottom end of High Street was adjudged too narrow for double lines, so this bit remained single. Getting so many trams along this and in and out of the Station Road terminus proved wholly impracticable on St Leger Day 1902, so the 1903 Order included two further additions. The spur at the Racecourse was turned into a loop and the High Street bottleneck was by-passed by means of a single line along Printing Office Street and Priory Place. Cars did not run into Station Road at all, but just kept going, scarcely pausing to drop off passengers before returning to pick up another load. Loop terminals like this were very rare in British practice and did not come into general use in Europe until single-ended trams became more common in the 1950s and 60s. So Doncaster was well ahead in this development. Incidentally, one driver had a memorable mishap at Station Road. Drivers were supposed to stop the car, get out, and change the points with the metal point iron carried on the tram. But they found that by driving on one notch of power and applying the hand brake, it was possible to lean out and change the point. However, this man leant too far, his watch fell out of his pocket, and the tram ran over it!

The Bentley line had, of course, to start at the far side of the level crossing in Marsh Gate, which was the only way across the East Coast Main Line at this period. A few trams, perhaps four, were kept just off Marsh Gate in an old barn standing on Corporation-owned land, where today's road maintenance depot is. This was evidently a flimsy building and blew down in a gale over the winter of 1904-5. It was replaced by a new shed for three cars. When the route first opened a shuttle car was run from Station Road to the level crossing at a supplementary fare of ½d. Passengers then walked through a subway to reach the waiting Bentley tram. However it did not take good Yorkshire folk long to realise that it was almost as easy and certainly cheaper to walk! So the shuttle was withdrawn after less than a fortnight. In December 1903 a tram was put on from the Guildhall on Friday nights and Saturday afternoons, this time at no extra charge, but this too was dropped after only two months. Plans for a bridge, known as the New or North Bridge (it is, of course, neither today), were finalised in 1908 and the tram rails required were obtained from Hull; few steel manufacturers would have been interested in rolling only 225 tons of the special type required. The bridge should have been formally opened on 12 May 1910, but due to the death of Edward VII, the ceremony was cancelled and the bridge thrown open to traffic on or just before that date. At last, through trams from Doncaster to Bentley were possible, luckily at almost the same time as production was beginning at the new Bentley colliery, which had been sunk during the period 1905-9.

To provide an even better service, it was decided to apply for powers to extend the line into New Village, which had been built for the pit workers. Authorised in 1911, the new line was completed by March 1913. On the 19th the track was inspected by Lt Col Druitt from the BOT. Their agreement had always to be obtained before opening any tramway, and services began the following day. All these changes resulted in a marked increase in the revenue on this route. £3,700 was taken in 1911 and by 1913 it was £6,160. It was probably by no means a coincidence that until 1912 the tramways' account, after servicing the capital, had only ever shown a small surplus in two years, but from 1913 onwards there was a continuous run of seven years during which the undertaking paid its way.

The trams' earning power was still further increased by the two wartime extensions to Warmsworth, a prolongation of the Balby route, and to Brodsworth. Both were again designed to serve collieries, and their construction would probably not have been permitted otherwise under wartime conditions. The Warmsworth terminus was rather inconveniently placed for its intended clientele, the miners at New Edlington. Tramwaymen tended to have a rather cavalier attitude to their passengers; 'they will walk across the gap as they always have', said one of a contemporary South Yorkshire proposal which also ignored the need for through services. Trams were, however, not to have the field to themselves for much longer. In fact, the construction of the Brodsworth line in particular was seriously questioned in 1911-12. The whole Tramways' Committee decided to visit the newly installed 'trackless trams', otherwise trolleybuses, in Bradford and Leeds. Evidently impressed, they agreed to reconsider the form of traction to Brodsworth and the whole Council only voted for trams by 11:7. The possibility of Corporation motor buses had been raised even earlier, in 1907, and were seriously proposed in 1913. Two councillors suggested buying six to eight to run to both Brodsworth and Edlington, though the Council voted this out by a larger margin. So in the event, both lines were built, the Brodsworth one being quite innovative in that most of it was laid on a reservation beside the Great North Road. This form of track was cheaper to build and maintain and also, of course, avoided any conflict with other traffic.

An early subject of controversy was whether or not to run trams on Sundays. A correspondent to a local paper in 1902 opined that anyone breaking the 4th commandment 'throws himself open to the wrath of the Eternal God'. What he would think of the average shopping centre today, I don't know! A town plebiscite in 1905 was 3:1 against the idea. In 1911 the Vicar of Balby said that even repairs to the track would be 'an organised trespass on the sacred rest of Sunday', and it was only on the outbreak of the First World War that Sunday services began, on 30 August 1914, from midday until 9 pm. Overcrowding was obviously becoming a problem - even before the war one 56 seat tram had been logged with 120 passengers! And from October 1915 the following bulky traffic was forbidden: fish in boxes, meat in bulk, fixed prams and mail carts. It's interesting to see what trams, with their capacious rear platforms, *could* take! After the conflict Sunday trams were withdrawn again in 1921, but this was due to a series of actual and threatened miners' and tramwaymens' strikes in the period 1918-21. The management had been rather pleased to find that Sunday trams made a profit and so petitions for their permanent withdrawal, such as that made in 1923 by the Band of Hope, received short shrift. On the other hand, the Committee were willing to consider making some travel concessions including, for instance, a free ride for the inmates of the workhouse at Balby for their monthly day's outing. In today's commercial world not many passengers get a free pass but, fortunately, few are so destitute as the residents in a workhouse. In 1920 uniformed police were given free passes, but this left a problem: what to do about plain clothes detectives? It was suggested they might have a distinctive badge to show to conductors, which rather missed the point about their undercover status.

Industrial relations were poor immediately after the war. Until 1914 drivers earned about 6d ($2\frac{1}{2}$p) an hour, conductors 1d less. Inflation and labour shortages during the war resulted in the payment of war bonuses, between two and three shillings (10-15p) and disputes arose afterwards about whether these should be consolidated into wages and whether the rates themselves should be increased or not. The Amalgamated Association of Tramway & Vehicle Workers and another union went on strike in March 1918 and, though some concessions were made, difficulties continued until the early Twenties. Labour discipline was harsh. In 1926 a crew was operating a miners' special to Brodsworth which involved a layover of half an hour, during which they bought some fish and chips. They were spotted eating them in uniform, and were dismissed. That was what gave the opportunity to sixteen-year-old Stanley Frith to get a job as a tram conductor. He himself was given seven days notice (later rescinded) twice, on the first occasion for failing to observe the custom of stopping (a motor bus this time) to pick up the Chairman of the Tramways Committee outside his front door. On another occasion when he was suspended for a week he left home religiously at 6.30 am each day so his grandma, who brought him up, wouldn't find out! Even joining in authorised recreations was not made easy. Stanley was in the tramways' football team, which played in the Thursday League. That meant a late turn on Wednesday until 11.30 pm, an early turn from 4.30 am till 2.00 pm, and a quick dash for the kick off at 2.30 pm. The job could be dangerous too. Once a trolley head fell on him, leading to a three week spell in hospital.

After the First World War it had been intended to continue with the policy of providing transport to outlying communities by tram and concrete plans were made for a line from the Racecourse to

Silver Street from Cleveland Street, Doncaster

Rossington. Ten new trams were ordered and an annexe to the depot planned to house them. Motor buses would have been used to provide connecting services. However, the deadline for making an application in 1919 was missed, and by the following year the success of rival motor bus firms made this form of transport an obvious contender for the long-distance routes. Early trolleybuses in Rotherham and York were inspected in 1921, but it was petrol buses which eventually introduced municipal services to new coalfield communities in 1922. It was too late to cancel the order for the extra trams, however, and both they and the depot annexe (sometimes referred to as the Car Repairing Shed) arrived in 1920. A later employee cannot actually recall trams using this shed, but this was probably after some trams had been withdrawn.

The tramway track and vehicles ended the war in a generally poor condition. A passenger complained about car 11 which 'could be felt to bulge out with every jolt [and]... must collapse shortly if not attended to'. During the war shortage of both materials and skilled staff exacerbated the maintenance backlog. Track repair had also been neglected and the inherent weakness of the initial construction had shown itself to disastrous effect. In one case the Council even threatened to close an entire route unless the Ministry of Munitions gave them permission to buy the necessary materials which, since it was the line to a colliery, they did. A journalist who sampled the first car to Warmsworth gave a superbly ironic impression of what the rest of the system was like. He was struck by 'the novel smoothness with which the car travelled – the absence of jolting, jumping over rough places, and that continual oscillation of every molecule of car structure... which sends a responsive vibration through the spinal column and is an invariable feature of travel on any other part of the Doncaster tramway system'. Travel along Nether Hall Road, part of which was actually to be re-laid in 1916 with a reinforced concrete foundation, was like a 'cross channel journey', with the tram pitching and rolling, like a ferry on a trip to Calais. Should the voyager be robbed of these sensations, he would 'have to seek them on the billows of the Bentley Road'.

Despite all this, the highest-ever profit was earned in 1919. This was highly illusory, however, because whilst traffic had been artificially boosted in the war years and income had risen, underlying costs were actually rising faster. A deficiency of the legislation under which tramways had been set up was that, in an era of stable prices, no provision had been made for increasing fares in an inflationary period, as wartime almost always is. Some relief was afforded by the *Tramways (Increase of Charges) Act* of 1920, though an undertaking still had to apply to raise its fares, which Doncaster did in the same year. A further problem exacerbated by the return to peace-time conditions was a huge increase in the number of competing motor buses, run either by medium-sized companies, such as Underwoods (which later became East Midlands Motor Services), or by a vast number of small proprietors. There was some legal protection available to tramways, but the small one-man concerns often ignored these restrictions. A rather more successful riposte was the introduction of an imaginative new fare structure in 1923, whereby passengers could buy weekly tickets over a certain distance permitting them to travel as often as they wished. This was a better solution than the pre-war workmen's fares which were offered at various times of day, because it 'captured' riders for a full week. It was this, together with a rapid fall in costs as prices fell from the post-war peak, which enabled a return to profitability for the trams in 1923-28 (except for the year of the General Strike). During this period a final addition to the network was authorised, a loop line via Factory Lane and Trafford Street, though in the event only the latter section was constructed as a terminus for the Bentley and Brodsworth cars. The extra crossover in the main line here had been laid in 1919 as an earlier attempt to make the reversing trams less obstructive. Plans were also made many times to double the Balby line, but only a small part was ever done. As a stopgap measure, Harveys Patent signals were installed on the section between Balby Church and Oswin Avenue in 1921.

By 1928, however, the first two tram routes had already closed. As the recovery of their fortunes in the 1920s shows, the tramways were not driven out of business by motor bus competition, ruinous though this appeared to the management at the time. Abandonment was due to several decisions taken as far back as the turn of the century. First, there was the temptation to build lines to areas with insufficient traffic potential. As well as the Oxford Street line, the Avenue Road route had never paid. An attempt to economise on its operation was made in 1917 when a small single-deck tram known as a demi-car was purchased from Erith Council. This was designed to be operated by a driver only and may possibly have done so for a while. But union pressure soon led to crew operation again, so the tram was withdrawn at an early date and was scrapped in 1925. Low traffic cannot pay for the fixed equipment required by a tramway, so if economies could not be made, the only solution was to close the tramway. Which was done in April 1925 when motor buses were used experimentally on a new service to Wheatley Hills via Avenue Road. Incidentally, this illustrates a further problem with established tramways; how to serve new housing built 'beyond the tracks'? Buses were not an unmitigated success, and by November it was clear that they were not coping with peak hour crowds. So it was decided to put a tram back at midday (at this period most workers went home for lunch) and tea time. Early in 1926 there was a proposal to reintroduce a full tram service to supplement the buses, but it was decided to improve the bus service instead. The trams may have stopped running then, though the tracks remained *in situ*, for in October 1926 the Department was prepared to charter a special tram from Woodlands to Avenue Road 'or at any rate as near to that point as possible'. However, there is a reference to a tram service on Avenue Road, and using one of the latest cars too, in March 1927. If accurate, this pushes the final closure even later.

The other route which closed whilst the system as a whole was still profitable was that to Bentley. Bentley Council, then separate from Doncaster, started complaining about the track in 1912, just ten years after construction. On average, tram track usually lasted about twenty years, so Doncaster's was clearly very badly constructed. The joints, the paving and especially the foundations gave constant trouble. This, then, was the second cause of closure. In 1916 a small section in Bentley was relayed, but the complaints continued. In 1922 the West Riding County Council said it wished to relay the road at a higher level, which would have meant moving the tracks. Doncaster decided in 1923 that it would not do this, but would abandon the tramway and substitute it with trolleybuses. This conclusion was reached not simply because the existing track was worn out, but because it would have been uneconomic to renew. There were, in turn, two reasons for this.

First, the forty year loans raised to finance the original construction still had twenty years to run. If new track had been built, a fresh loan would have had to be raised. Whereas the earnings could cover the old loans, they could never have financed both. Whether asset life was grossly over-estimated or if the Borough Treasurer's desire to spread the loans over as long a period as possible was at fault is immaterial; reconstruction was uneconomic. The Manager, Mr Potts, reported that 'It is this, and this alone, which makes it difficult to [put] the undertaking in good running order, without being a charge on the rates'. A second problem was that capital costs were much higher post-war than they had been in 1900. Within a year, the obvious conclusion had been drawn. If it was not worth reconstructing one of the most profitable tram routes, it was not worth saving the others either. This was particularly so when two final factors were borne in mind. The existing single-line tram tracks were quite unsuitable for modern traffic conditions. And, as Avenue Road had shown, extensions were necessary anyway. So, as a report presented by the Manager demonstrated, it was not simply a question of replacing the existing tramway; it would have needed complete modernisation and lengthy extensions, both of which would have left the undertaking seriously overcapitalised. So a trackless, and cheaper, alternative was to be pursued.

In summary, therefore, the Doncaster tramways closed for the following reasons: they were badly built, some routes were uneconomic, there was a continuing debt, the cost of new construction was too high, complete reconstruction and expansion was required and, finally, there were alternatives, which there had not been in 1902.

It had not yet been finally decided whether to use trolley or motor buses, but experience with Avenue Road evidently persuaded the Council to go for the former. So general powers for trolleybuses were obtained in the *Doncaster Corporation Act* 1926. The installation work went to Clough, Smith & Co. The Bentley conversion involved the reconstruction of the tramway overhead with double wires (because trolleybuses cannot send return current through the tracks), an extension in the form of a one-way loop around New Village and a loop at the town end to get buses from the depot to the North Bridge terminus. An extension to Toll Bar was also authorised, but this was never built. There were still ideas at this time of serving other colliery villages with trolleybuses too, such as Armthorpe, Edlington (as an extension of the Warmsworth tram route) and Brodsworth (another tramway replacement), but only the Edlington branch was authorised and all actually became motor bus routes. Trolleybus 1 was delivered in April 1928 and was used for driver training on the Racecourse road, presumably so as not to hinder the conversion work in Bentley. The route itself opened on 22 August 1928 and was an immediate success. Revenue rose by 50 per cent over the trams to Bentley and averaged 38 per cent over later conversions. Trolleybuses were faster than the trams, larger, quieter, much more comfortable, virtually silent, able to load at the kerb edge and, as opposed to motor buses, cheaper to run (though not, of course, to install). Potts felt that trolleybuses with their fast acceleration were ideally suited for town traffic, and it was precisely on these urban routes that they were employed. They possess, he thought, 'the efficiency, reliability and safety of the Tramcar, without the inherent drawback of being track bound', though he did recognise that trams were better able to cope with peaks such as football traffic. At the time (the mid-1920s) he felt that petrol buses were not up to the job and in his experience had a 'useful life not over four years when [there was] a lot of stopping and starting'. Diesel engines were just being experimented with, but he was able to find a hostage to fortune in Sir Herbert Austin who believed that 'a crude oil engine could never be a success in any Motor Omnibus'. After the conversion, Doncaster Corporation Transport (DCT) was consistently profitable, so much so that by the late 1930s the Department was able to ignore the Council and the Borough Treasurer and could afford to buy new vehicles etc. out of revenue without needing loan sanction. This was not popular in the corridors of power!

Stanley Frith says that the trolleybuses were the nicest vehicles he ever drove. But they did have their downsides. Once he was driving the last bus back from Wheatley Hills. It always ran straight through without stopping, but he went that bit too fast, his trolleys flew off the wires and brought all the overhead down, even managing to cut off the electricity to the neighbouring houses!

Tom Potts was definitely a character, though probably one better appreciated in retrospect. Faced with the problem of peak hour overcrowding, he wondered why passengers refused to stagger their journeys. Why should the Department have 'to move a mass of people who adopt such stupid and sheep-like methods?' His opinion of his staff was no higher. He wrote to a complainant, 'I have to inform you that I am satisfied the information was furnished by a member of my staff, but like many other concerns I employ a number of half wits'! And the Ministry of Transport did not escape his tongue. 'The queries raised... suggest the urgent necessity for the provision of other playgrounds for Civil Servants.' Some problems do not change, however. Shelters, he said, are 'expensive to maintain, nearly impossible to keep clean, and quite impossible to prevent being abused'.

This to to run ahead of the story though. The other routes are listed in Table 2. The Wheatley Hills motor bus service was changed to trolleybuses and slightly extended in 1931. It was unique in using red-lettered destination blinds. One story has it that a councillor asked for help in recognising his bus after leaving the pub! Though the truth is more prosaic, because Potts would have liked a general colour system; it was just that none of the others showed up properly. According to some sources, buses were used temporarily on other routes whilst the conversion of the overhead was completed, but there is no real evidence for this, except for the Racecourse section. The Beckett Road route was extended a bit beyond the tram tracks to find space for the trolleybuses to turn, though there still wasn't room for a loop, only for a reversing wye. The other new section was a continuation along Carr House Lane, and from then on the Hyde Park and Racecourse services were operated as an inner and outer circle. As already mentioned, it had been planned to run out to Edlington, but this was outside the Borough and various legal problems meant that the matter was left in abeyance. Because of low bridges single deck trolleybuses would have had to be used too. The Balby route was therefore actually cut back from Warmsworth to the Borough boundary, where a temporary terminus with a wye was provided down a side street.

Harold Green used to take a ha'penny ride from the Balby Cinema to town during this changeover period and would sit on the open balcony of the tram, watching the trolley passing under the overhead. The tram wires were strung over the single line and at some stops would not part company at the loops, so the trolleys of inward-bound cars were at full stretch. On reaching St Sepulchre Gate the Balby trams used the positive trolleybus wire for short distances. Depot bound trolleybuses would often pull across French Gate whilst the conductor yanked the trolleys off their wires. The bus would stop on the crown of the (Great North!) road whilst one trolley was re-attached to the single tram wire and a 'skate' was attached to run in the rail groove so the journey to the depot could be completed. Later, of course, trolleybus wires were installed on this section. During conversion of the Balby route the trams used the new wiring until the trolleybuses took over. In this case, as in some others, at least one experimental run was made on the Sunday prior to the changeover.

Table 2
TROLLEYBUS ROUTES

Route	Opened	Extended	Closed
Bentley	22 Jun 1928	–	12 Feb 1956
Hexthorpe	1 Jul 1929	–	17 Mar 1962
Beckett Rd	31 Jul 1929	Apr 1941 & 17 Feb 1958	14 Dec 1963
Hyde Park	16 Jan 1930	–	10 Dec 1961
Racecourse	20 Mar 1930	–	30 Dec 1963
Wheatley Hills	4 Mar 1931	14 Oct 1958	30 Dec 1962
Balby	26 Jul 1931	Jul 1942	8 Sep 1962

The Brodsworth tramway soldiered on until 1935 to wear out the assets, which it did! Two cars caught fire during April 1935, one being partially destroyed (presumably 40, as in the case of 47 'Major

Permain assisted with his fire extinguisher'). According to Potts, writing in 1935, 'the most antique thing in the neighbourhood is the tramway system'. Eight trams were sold for scrap, but only four were runners, so it is probable that both motor buses and trams were used from 23 March 1935 until final replacement by the latter.

All the pre-war trolleybuses were large and elegant three-axle vehicles, mostly Karriers, though the first four were built by Garretts and one (a unique vehicle) was one of only two Bristol trolleybuses ever built. A trial was made with a white-liveried Leyland demonstrator early in 1935, but according to the Manager, they never got a full day's service out of it. Unlike the Bristol Company, though, Leyland persevered with the trolleybuses and supplied a number of operators. Doncaster's bodies were nearly always by Roe's of Leeds, despite Potts' acerbic comment over delivery delays. 'It may well be that when your reorganisation is complete that your customers will enjoy some consideration, but there is not the slightest doubt that if we continue to be treated in this fashion, we shall not remain customers.' The design was gradually refined and simplified up to 1939. Mr Potts was an enthusiast for the three-axle design, though maintenance costs were probably higher than for two-axle vehicles. He had to buy some of the latter during the war, because that is all there was, and his successor, Mr Bamford, preferred them anyway. He replaced and renewed the fleet by buying second-hand buses and then giving most of them standardised modern bodies, again by Roe. He was very good when it came to mechanical matters. Once three Sheffield motor buses destined for scrap were shedded overnight in Doncaster and Bamford seized the opportunity to swop some parts over!

Strangely imitating the First World War, there were two extensions made during the Second World War, one further along Beckett Road and the other to Barrel Lane, Balby. In both cases the cramped turning facilities could be replaced by loops. An option not available in the Great War was to fit loudspeakers in the trolleybuses to announce the stops in the blackout. Conductors needed torches to collect fares at night and were given a battery allowance. For the driver, it made little difference if the headlamps were on or off, making driving very difficult. Drivers were exempt from call-up, incidentally. If there was an air raid warning, the bus was stopped and the trolleys tied down until the 'all clear'. In 1940 two scrap vehicles were loaned to the local Defence Volunteers, Dad's Army, for use as barriers, mimicking the use to which trams were put to in earnest in Germany five years later.

Expansion continued in the post-war period and powers were obtained for three extensions in 1958, one to the Beckett Road route, one further out from Wheatley Hills and a completely new branch off the Balby route to Broomhouse Lane; the latter was not built, and the new service was started with motor buses on 14 September 1959. In fact, the days of electric transport were numbered. Electricity nationalisation in the 1940s meant that municipalities no longer had an interest in supplying power to their own undertaking and, as Doncaster found, often had to pay higher rates for their current. As other systems closed, the supply of new trolleybuses dried up. The cost of installing the overhead rose sharply to between £8,000 and £10,000 a mile, putting trolleybuses in the same position as trams had been a generation earlier. And Doncaster was beginning its long career as a compulsive road builder, which meant that old street patterns were being broken and the trolleybus wiring would have had to change not once but several times. Some attempt was made to adapt by, for instance, running the buses around the then-new roundabout at the Racecourse, but even this small change required the planting of eighteen new poles. Town centre changes to cope with new one-way systems were proposed but never implemented. And, again like the trams, the trolleybus routes were not serving newer areas of the town. The Bentley route, once again, was the first to close, in 1955; once again too, there was a particular reason for this, the long-term reconstruction of the Mill Bridge. But despite the minor additions in 1958, the last trolleybus ran surprisingly soon after that, on 14 December 1963. Nine years later the current for the last trolleybus system of all in the UK, at Bradford, to which a handful of the Doncaster vehicles had migrated, was turned off. Except for the Blackpool sea-front tramway, an era was over.

That was not the end of electric transport in the area though. One trolleybus, 375, was preserved and has run at the Sandtoft Museum in North Lincolnshire. And in 1985 a test track was opened along the Racecourse to demonstrate a new generation of trolleybus which South Yorkshire Passenger Transport Executive had hopes of reintroducing to both Doncaster and Rotherham. Unfortunately, bus deregulation made investment in fixed track modes like this seem unattractive, and the bus itself has ended up at Sandtoft too. Even so, it is still possible to travel under the wires to Bentley and to near Brodsworth, because after the Doncaster-Leeds railway line was electrified, new stations were opened at Bentley and Adwick, served today by modern electric multiple units. So, a century after the first trams started running, a journey from Station Road via North Bridge to Bentley can still be achieved, and with some of the same sounds and motion; even if it is a bit quicker than it was!

Trams & Trolleybuses

By 1901 many towns, such as Leeds and Sheffield, had electric tramways on which the Doncaster system might have been modelled. But the Council sent a delegation to nearby Hull and decided on their unique form of rail, which had a groove in the centre instead of to one side, the idea being to give a smoother ride. This early picture of Carr Lane in Hull shows another special feature, the use of trailer trams, which was swiftly found to be inefficient and was never contemplated for Doncaster. In later years the two Corporations often placed joint orders for track or, in Doncaster's case, borrowed from the larger authority. *Author's collection*

One of the few places where centre-groove track can still be seen is outside Wheeler Street tram depot on Anlaby Road in Hull. Hull's track was laid on a concrete slab and paved either in stone setts, like this example, or with wooden blocks. For cost reasons, the Doncaster track had setts only along each parallel rail and either a narrow concrete strip underneath this or a thin concrete bed (it is not quite clear which), false economy which caused untold trouble later on. The first rails were received on 12 September 1901. *The author*

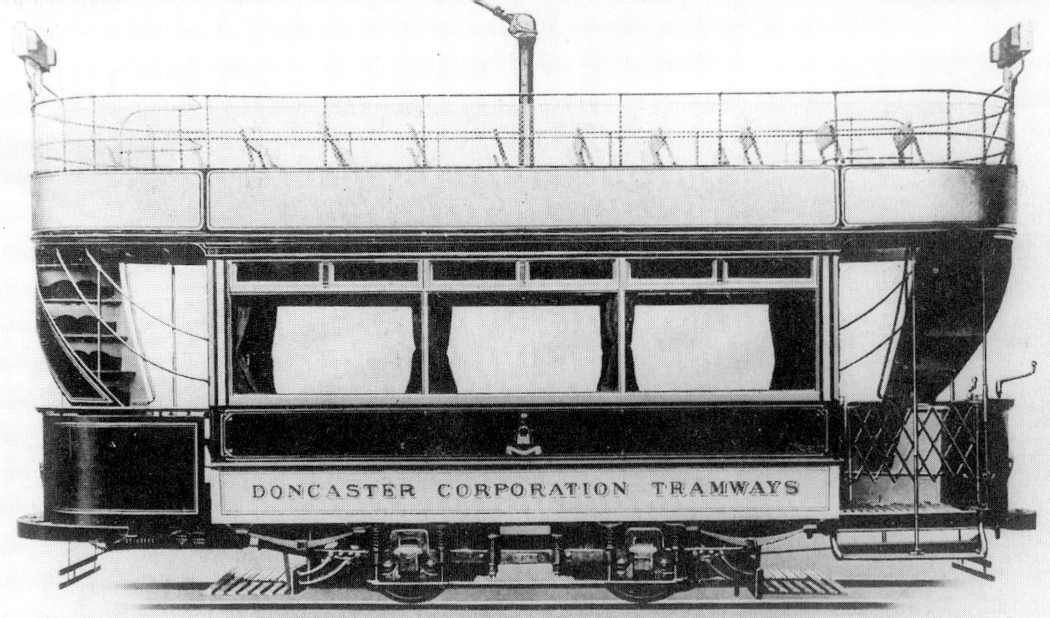

Doncaster's first trams were to have been single-deck, but it was quickly decided to order a standard design of double-decker with four wheels (a single truck) rather than bogies and an open top deck. This builder's photograph clearly shows the lifeguard, a wooden tray which fell to pick up anyone unfortunate enough to be on the track and to 'trip' the wooden slats hanging down at the front; or at least, that was the theory! Doncaster's first trams were quite 'posh', with curtains and a length of carpet along the lower deck seats; neither feature lasted long. *Charles Hall collection*

The tramways were built partly to provide a large customer for the new municipal electric power station, so it was natural to appoint the manager of the latter to run the trams too. That was Mr Wyld (in office 1902-4), seen here on the front platform of tram number 1. The livery was described as Midland (Railway) Red and cream with gilt lettering and numerals. The car is outside the depot in Greyfriars Road; the power station was across the road. The area is roughly where the supermarket opposite St George's Church is today. *Author's collection*

On 2 June 2002 a ceremonial re-enactment of the opening of the tramways took place at the Mansion House. A number of vintage vehicles paraded here and at a later rally. In 1902 the Mayor walked from the Mansion House to the depot, opened it with a gold key, and then drove the first tram using a special silver plated controller handle. 2 June was a national holiday to celebrate the end of the Boer War, so this patriotically bedecked tram is being mobbed by eager crowds as it stands at the terminus in Station Road. *Author's collection*

❖

Still in Station Road (now entirely covered by the French Gate Centre, apart from the old Grand Theatre), the tram is now moving off towards St Sepulchre Gate. Only the lines to Hexthorpe and Balby were opened on the first day. *Author's collection*

A further tram ordered in 1902 was this water car and sweeper. It could brush snow from the tracks, but its main purpose was to dampen and sweep the dusty roads of the day. The brushes were driven by a third electric motor. It was fitted with 'Jarrards rail scrapers' for keeping the grooves free of debris. An old York horse tram was also acquired as a salt and sand trailer. *Charles Hall collection*

Neither of these pictures are particularly clear, but they are included for their interest. In this view the works car is following a passenger tram across the junction at Clock Corner. It looks at though the track has already been watered along St Sepulchre Gate, so the driver will probably reverse and follow one of the other roads. This was the only place in Doncaster where there were tracks going in four directions. *Charles Hall collection*

This is the top end of Station Road, with the Grand Theatre in the background and the Doncaster Mutual Industrial Co-operative Society's imposing premises on the left. Tram 3 is heading for Balby and is followed by number 16, delivered in 1903. This was the only appreciable section of double track on the original system, apart from the Racecourse route. *Charles Hall collection*

If the photographer had stayed on the same spot and turned to the right, this would have been the picture in his viewfinder. The small hut in the foreground was used by the tramway staff. It was removed in 1917 and replaced by an office and staff rest-room nearby. The single line along here was used by all except the two services which did not terminate in Station Road, a serious problem when road traffic began to increase a couple of decades later. Hardly any of the shop premises survive today. *Charles Hall collection*

Car 6 on the Balby section, but on a through service to Beckett Road, introduced (together with Avenue Road – Hexthorpe) in 1904. Bentley was also linked to the Racecourse for a brief period in 1910. The experiment was finally abandoned in 1917 because of unbalanced traffic. There remained some workmen's through cars, though, mostly to the later terminus at Brodsworth. This is quite a late view because the tram has a top cover which it may not have acquired until 1913. At this time the *Sheffield Telegraph* was a daily paper. *David Packer collection*

The Balby service terminated here, at Oswin Avenue. Car 5 is just arriving and the man sitting in the tramway shelter will board for the return trip to the town centre. As originally constructed, there were not enough passing loops, and on Saturday nights pairs of trams had to be run to Balby and Bentley to clear the crowds. *Charles Hall collection*

St. James's Church, Doncaster

Churches and pubs are often the only constants in street scenes, which is certainly the case for St James' church here. This part of St Sepulchre Gate and Cleveland Street has long been cut off from the rest of the town by the ring road. A Balby tram disappears townwards and on the left is the incline up to St James' Bridge, used by trams going to Hexthorpe. In 1904 a third tram route was opened to the right, to Oxford Street. Most of the foreground of this postcard scene is now the dual carriageway along Cleveland Street. *Charles Hall collection*

❖

Old Hexthorpe had quite a rural feel in the first decade of the last century. The date has to be between about 1906 and 1911, after through tram services began (number 16 will be returning to Avenue Road) and before the early white blinds were replaced by black ones. The two track layout was typical of most terminals, but the second track can rarely have been needed, given the service frequency. The children are enjoying posing for the photographer. *David Packer collection*

The Hexthorpe route was good tramway territory, passing through closely packed streets of terraced houses built to house workers at the Plant Works. The tram heading out of the town is one of the original twenty-five open-toppers, but with a later top cover. The centre-groove rail is clearly visible, as are the typical curlicues on the overhead bracket.

The white band painted on the pole indicates a request stop, which is just past Salisbury Road. This part of the street is now called Urban Road, after a period in which is was known as Sunnyside to match a parallel road, Shadyside. The big house behind the railings has been replaced by a pair of semi-detached houses. *Dancerama/Old Barnsley*

One of the first twenty trams, perhaps 19, is still unsullied by advertisements, which were first permitted in 1903. It has just turned the corner from St Sepulchre Gate and is on its way up High Street past the imposing bank building on the right. This was the only length of single track on the Racecourse route, and though perfectly adequate for the normal light service was shown by the first race days in 1902 to be a major bottleneck when an intensive service was required. *David Packer collection*

The Mansion House was where the double line began. Beyond here, High Street was too narrow, so additional powers were obtained in 1903 to add a single loop line along Priory Place and Printing Office Street, plus a turning circle at the racecourse end, meaning that trams could be 'run in one continuous circle, one after the other without changing the trolley pole'. *Charles Hall collection*

The Racecourse route had the only continuous length of double track. This is a fine view of the elegant South Parade, a reminder of Doncaster's time as a centre of high fashion in the eighteenth century. The tramway layout was purely for the races, otherwise the line never paid and could be operated by only a couple of trams. At its peak, 250,000 punters arrived on St Leger Day, and though the tramways could never carry more than a quarter of them, many extra trams were laid on, for instance to meet the Great Central (GC) race specials at St James' Sidings. Because the system was officially a light railway, first class fares of 6d (2^{1}/$_{2}$p) could be charged as against the usual 1d. *Author's collection*

The passengers are enjoying a summer day on the open top of car 14 as it passes along Bennetthorpe; beyond here there were no houses at all until the Racecourse was reached. Only a horse cart and a couple of bicycles disturb the dust on the macadamised road, and there were few customers for the trams. All this despite the fact that the line lay along the Great North Road; the glory days of the coaching era were behind it and the motor age was yet to come. *David Packer collection*

The overhead wires, one for each direction of travel, were neatly installed by Messrs Blackwell and hung on cast-iron poles, which were painted light green with dark green bases.

The tram, running on its single line down the centre of Balby High Road, is just about opposite the *Plough Inn*. Today, this is the A630 and one half of a busy dual carriageway; the chapel and all the property on the right has been cleared to make way for the new road layout. The ground level fell away rapidly here, so the chapel had a large schoolroom beneath it. The low building beyond it was a toll house and later did duty as the Balby Library.
Author's collection

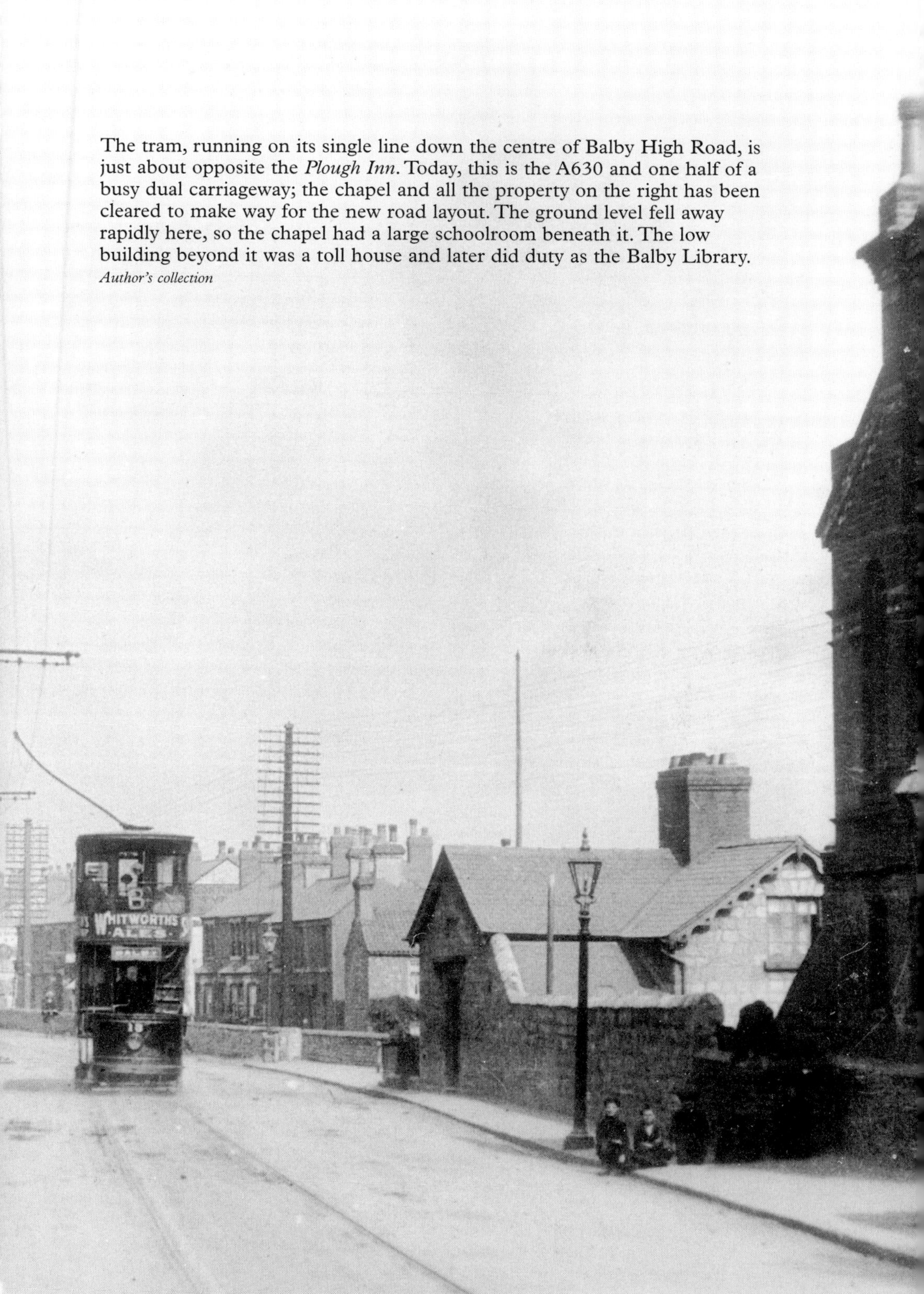

The original print of 22 had clearly seen better days, but it is a splendid view of the tram and its crew in their regulation caps and greatcoats. In open-top form these cars had what were known as reversed stairs, which had the disadvantage of obstructing the driver's view to the left. At night the top deck was illuminated only by the lamps at either end just underneath the destination boxes. The two brackets immediately below this would have been used for the route letters, but their use had been discontinued by the time the photograph was taken, probably on the Hyde Park route at the top of Spring Gardens.
Author's collection

Another view of a through Balby-Beckett Road car on route 'B' at Clock Corner, about to turn into Baxter Gate, and on its way to the latter terminus. Avenue Road trams shared the same route as far as Nether Hall Road. The latter was an unsuccessful line, being too short and serving a middle-class area where residents had their own transport. Another peculiarity of Doncaster's trams in the early days was the use of destination blinds with black lettering on a white background, instead of the more usual white on black.
Charles Hall collection

Number 3 is going to Hyde Park. It is standing on St Sepulchre Gate at the junction with Station Road. The overhead wiring here was supported on span wires, relatively uncommon in Doncaster, and the one in the foreground has what was known as a feeder cable running along it. The overhead lost voltage with distance, so every half mile or so this was boosted from higher capacity cables buried under the tracks; hence the feeder. The imposing tower of St George's parish church rises over the town. The church was designed by Sir George Scott to replace a medieval one destroyed by fire in 1853. *Charles Hall collection*

The crew waiting at the Oxford Street terminus are wearing the original style of uniform with pill box hats, superceded in 1904. The route, opened in 1903, was far too short to serve any useful purpose and the service was quickly restricted to peak periods only. The trams stopped altogether in July and thereafter ran only for a month's trial at half fare in the spring of 1907. The last tram of all ran on 18 May. Some of the track was dismantled and used elsewhere during the First World War, but the last was not lifted until 1925. *Author's collection*

The route to Bentley had to be operated in isolation because of the then level crossing, so the terminus was on the far side in Marsh Gate. When the new North Bridge was opened in 1910 the rails could be connected up. The new track was fully instead of partially paved, which was an improvement. There were complaints from the Carters' Association in 1920 about passengers throwing missiles at the horses; vandalism is nothing new! *Author's collection*

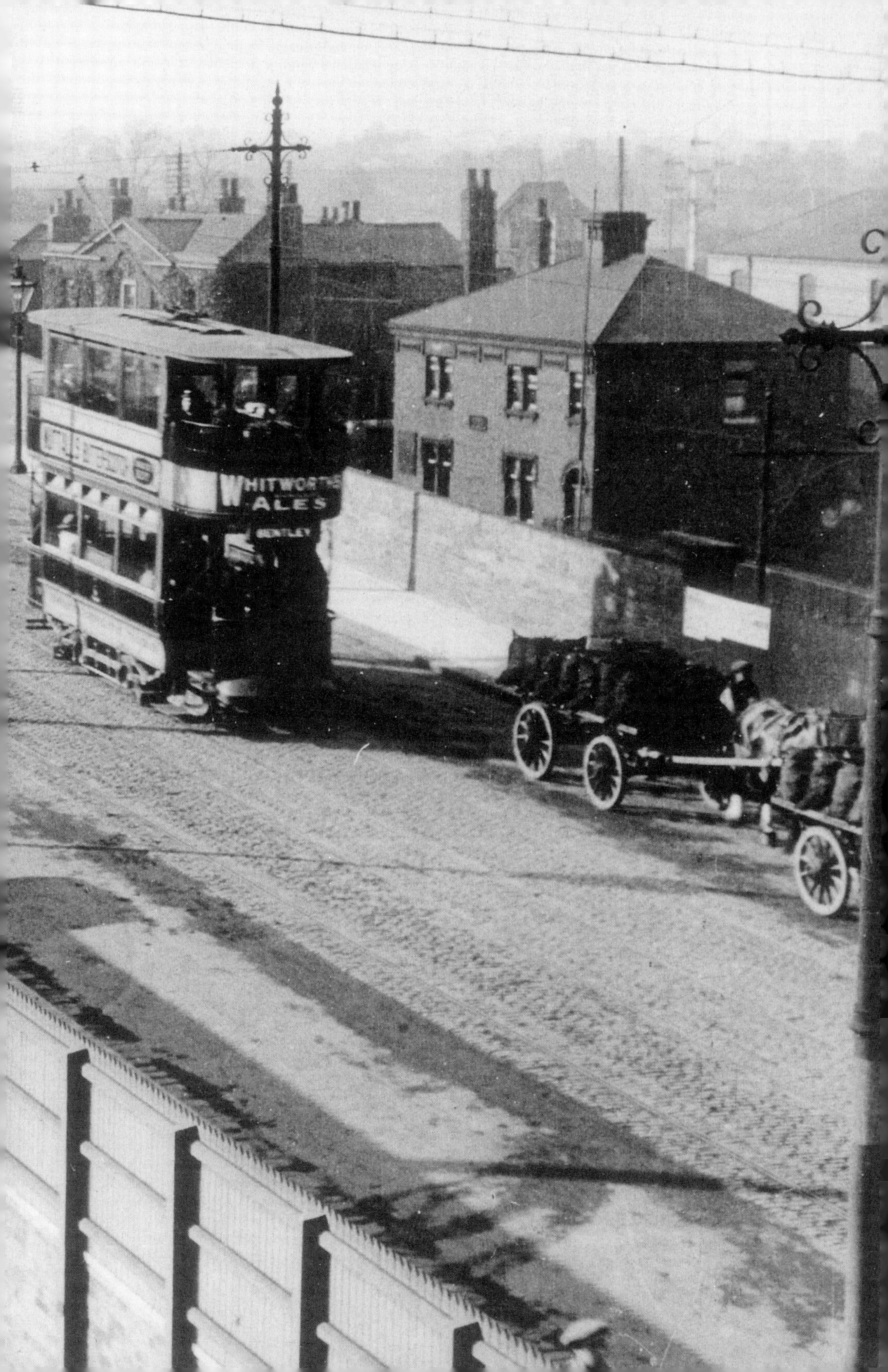
WHITWORTHS
ALES
BENTLEY

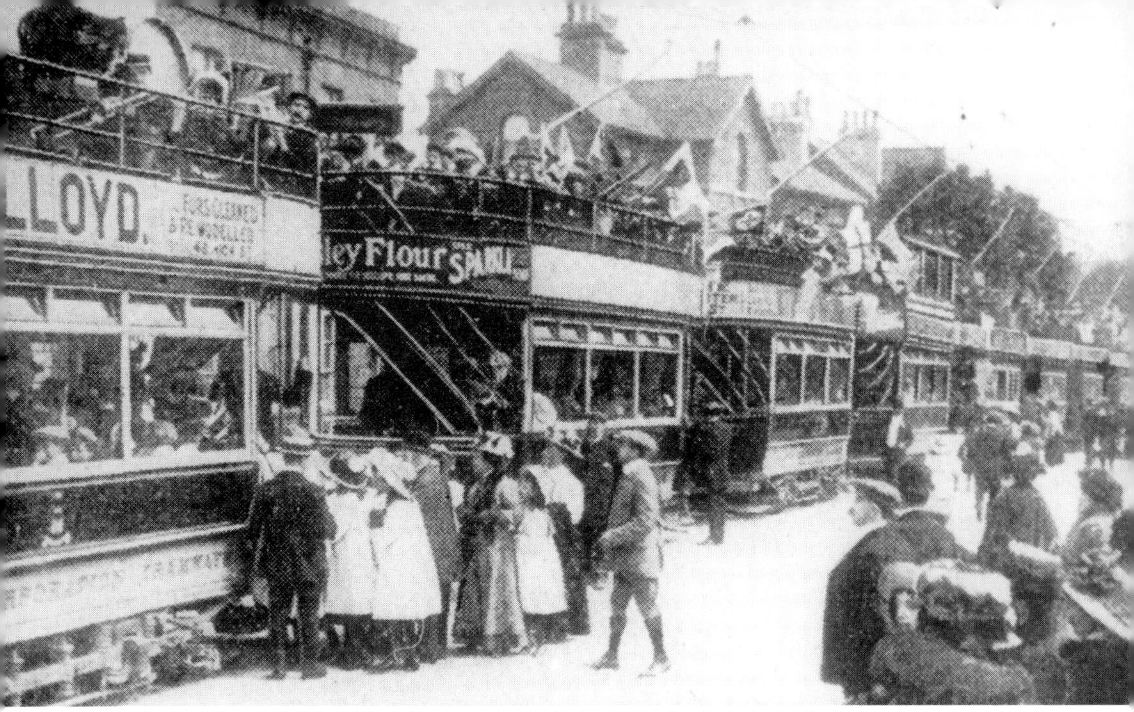

This major public celebration may have been Empire Day, which was a big event in the Edwardian period. Trams were also hired for local events, such as Sunday School outings. The date must be after 1907, when the first top covers were supplied, but not long after, given that all except one car is still open-topped. The era was a confident one, in which technological progress seemed to promise sustained progress, of which tramways appeared to be a good example. *Author's collection*

The ceremonial opening of the North bridge had to be deferred because of the death of Edward VII. When George V was crowned in the following year, a tram was decorated to mark the event. Car 21 was always used for such purposes and was one of those which kept its open top deck until withdrawal. It is standing on the turning circle at the Racecourse. The tradition of decorated vehicles, often with coloured lights like this, was something which began with electric trams and largely ended with the demise of the trolleybus, as an abundant source of energy was required. Number 21 was also used for overhead repairs on the later sleeper track to Brodsworth. *Author's collection*

This picture shows car 13 standing at the point where the track across the North Bridge singled again, near the junction with the depot line from Greyfriars Road. After 1910 this became the terminus for Bentley trams. The handsome portico behind the tram belonged to the Guildhall, unfortunately one of the casualties of Doncaster's redevelopment; one might be tempted to say, 'the many casualties', because respect for the past has not been the first thing one associates with successive Councils. This site is now occupied by Marks & Spencer. The second building along is the *White Swan* pub. Opposite is the Regal Cinema, popularly known as the 'Bug House' because of its profusion of uninvited patrons! *David Packer collection*

Car 8 looks very smart, possibly just after having its new top cover added. It is nearing the end of the new double line at the far side of the North Bridge, on its way out to Bentley. The tower of St George's is visible over the buildings in the background (a 'horse repository' was presumably a stables). The street on the other side of the *Bridge Hotel* is Marsh Gate, the site of the original Bentley tramway and its temporary depot. *David Packer collection*

Doncaster's first industrial base was the railway, its second was coal mining. The new townships which developed around the pits were, inevitably, some distance from the town itself, and transport for them was a major concern. The original Bentley village terminus in Chapel Street was some way short of the colliery, opened in 1908. So in 1913 an extension was added to the pit village, known as New Bentley. In 1918 Rayner, the Tramways' manager after 1904, floated the idea of running coal trams from the pit heads to the power station to save on the costs of cartage and transhipment, but nothing came of this. Here a tram approaches the Mill Bridge, a short way past the former terminus. *Charles Hall collection*

42

Car 24 is standing on the last passing loop in New Bentley at the Avenue and Arksey Lane. The shabby and battered appearance of the tram makes this a wartime view. Repainting ceased and accident damage was not repaired. Spares were virtually unobtainable and eventually some trams had to be cannibalised to provide parts to keep the others running. many staff joined the forces and so in July 1915, the first four conductresses were engaged to join what had formerly been an all-male workforce. The transparent destination indicators in the lower saloon windows were a Doncaster speciality; so was Nuttall's Butter-Scotch.

David Packer collection

The next series of trams was delivered in 1916 and was rather larger than the standard car with four windows per side and seating for 66 passengers. It had been found possible to squeeze an extra foot out of the Peckham trucks too. Rayner designed and patented these 'Kleencar' seats, which were fitted to 33-6. The longitudinal benches were usually panelled in and made sweeping the saloon awkward. *Tramway & Railway World*

The new type were supported by sprung legs and could be raised before the cleaners started work. It was also pointed out that people could tuck their feet under the seats and stow parcels there, freeing the floor area for standing passengers. The Peckham Company marketed the seats, which were taken up by a few other operators, including Ilford and Sheffield. *Tramway & Railway World*

Double-Decked Canopy-Top Car for Doncaster Corporation

Length of Car Body, 16 ft; Length overall, 28 ft 6 in.

Mounted upon a Peckham Patent P-22 Pendulum Truck

Wheel Base, 7 ft 6 in; Effective Wheel Base, 9 ft 6 in; Spring Base, 16 ft.

Cars 26–31 were ordered just before the war in this open balcony form with so-called direct stairs; older rebuilt trams also received these. The livery was slightly restyled, with cream panels around the upper deck instead of a continuous band. The Peckham P-22 trucks were of an improved type, again retro-fitted to up to five of the older cars. It will be obvious by now that the standard Doncaster, indeed British, tram had four wheels on a rigid wheelbase. It was impossible to lengthen the truck much more because of the difficulty of getting round bends in the track, and so the body, size and capacity (they had fifty-eight seats) was restricted too.

Charles Hall collection

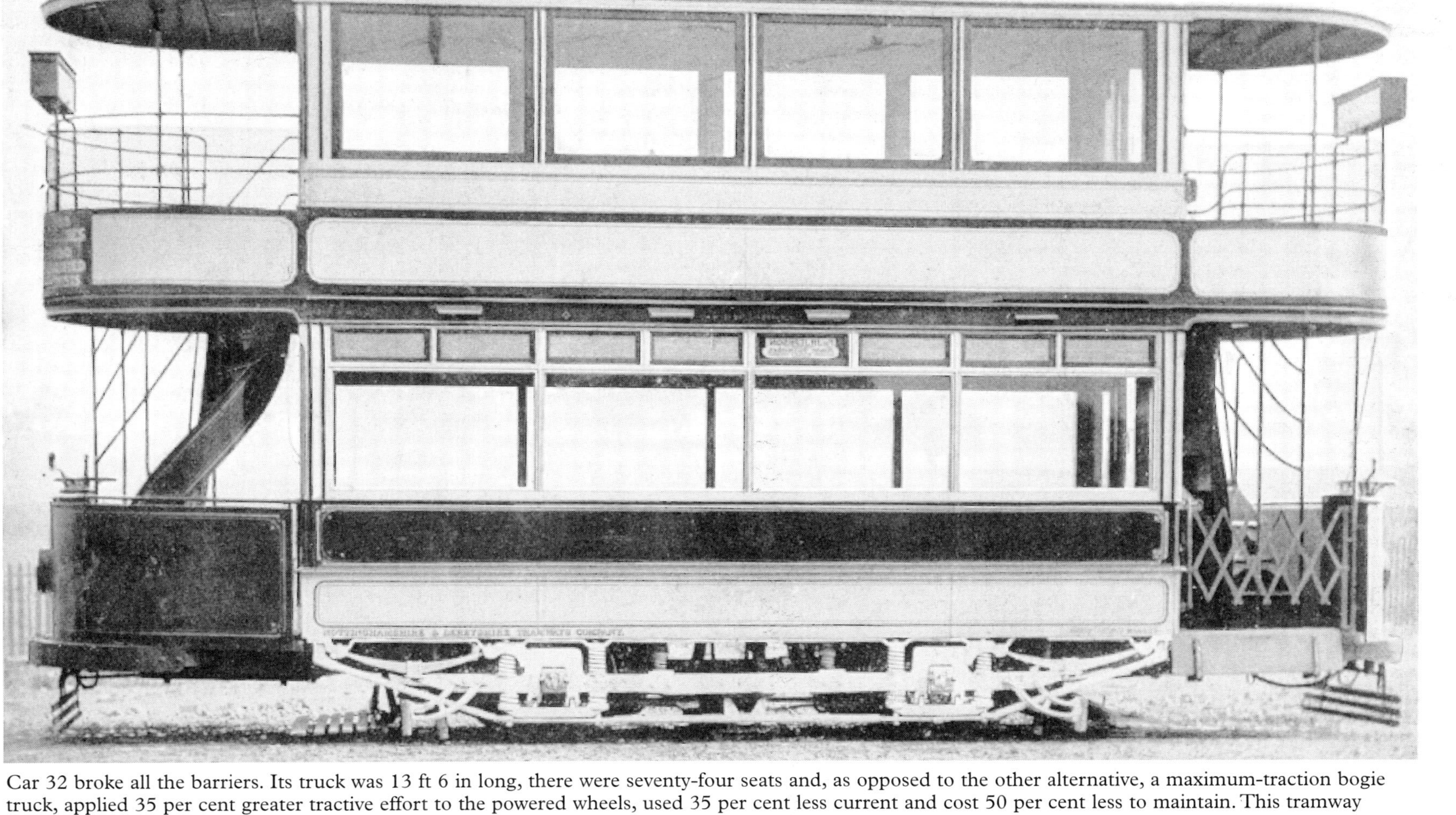

Car 32 broke all the barriers. Its truck was 13 ft 6 in long, there were seventy-four seats and, as opposed to the other alternative, a maximum-traction bogie truck, applied 35 per cent greater tractive effort to the powered wheels, used 35 per cent less current and cost 50 per cent less to maintain. This tramway philosopher's stone was known as a radial truck, the individual wheel sets being able to swivel independently of each other. Why was it the only one in the Doncaster (or almost any) tramway fleet? Because despite the manager's claim that the wheels returned 'to the parallel without any trouble', they didn't, but obstinately faced in different directions. Not unnaturally, the tram was rarely used until fitted with a conventional truck. Staff referred to it as 'Big Ben'. Another peculiarity, also later standardised, was the large driver's brake wheel, as opposed to the more usual handle. *Charles Hall collection*

Available sources differ on whether 33-36 had 'Kleencar' seats on their top decks too, but the next series of trams certainly did. This was quite a neat arrangement for transverse or 'garden' seats, whereby the whole of the seat could be folded up and clipped out of the way for cleaning. As with any seats of this pattern, the backs were moveable and were always reversed at the terminus so that passengers were facing the direction of travel. Such 'cross seating' was feasible on either deck of a tram, but in Doncaster was confined to the top. The floor was made of wood with slats attached in places of maximum wear. Beyond the saloon is the open balcony, which had a semi-circular seat on it; a favourite spot for generations of schoolboys! The young Harold Green used to like sitting at the rear to watch the trolley negotiate the various junctions. The poster advertises an alteration of fares. During and after the war fares had to be raised quite steeply to meet increased costs. *Charles Hall collection*

Rayner was a capable engineer and was seconded to the Admiralty during 1917-18. After the war he was appointed to the managership at Hull. Here he designed an experimental lightweight tram which dispensed with the usual separate truck. A model was produced, but only one full size car, partly because of Rayner's fraught relationship with the Hull councillors, which eventually led in 1930-31 to his dismissal on charges of using Corporation petrol for his own car. Tommy Potts, Rayner's successor at Doncaster, used religiously to store all his fuel receipts in a desk drawer. 'No-one is going to say, Missee, that I use the Department's petrol', he would say to his secretary (all female stall were 'Missee', whether sixteen or sixty years old). *The author*

Car 27, suffering severely from lack of maintenance, is pictured at Oswin Avenue during the First World War. The headlamp is masked as a defence against Zeppelin raids (several people had been killed by one in Sheffield in 1916). By now conductresses had been joined by women drivers, the first of whom was passed out in March 1916. Nobody knew what to call such a new species; should it be motorwoman, motoress or plain driver? Rayner said that suitable women had the nerve and quick reactions to do the work well. However, one was dismissed within less than two months after colliding successively with a horse dray, the paint shops and a furniture van!

Author's collection

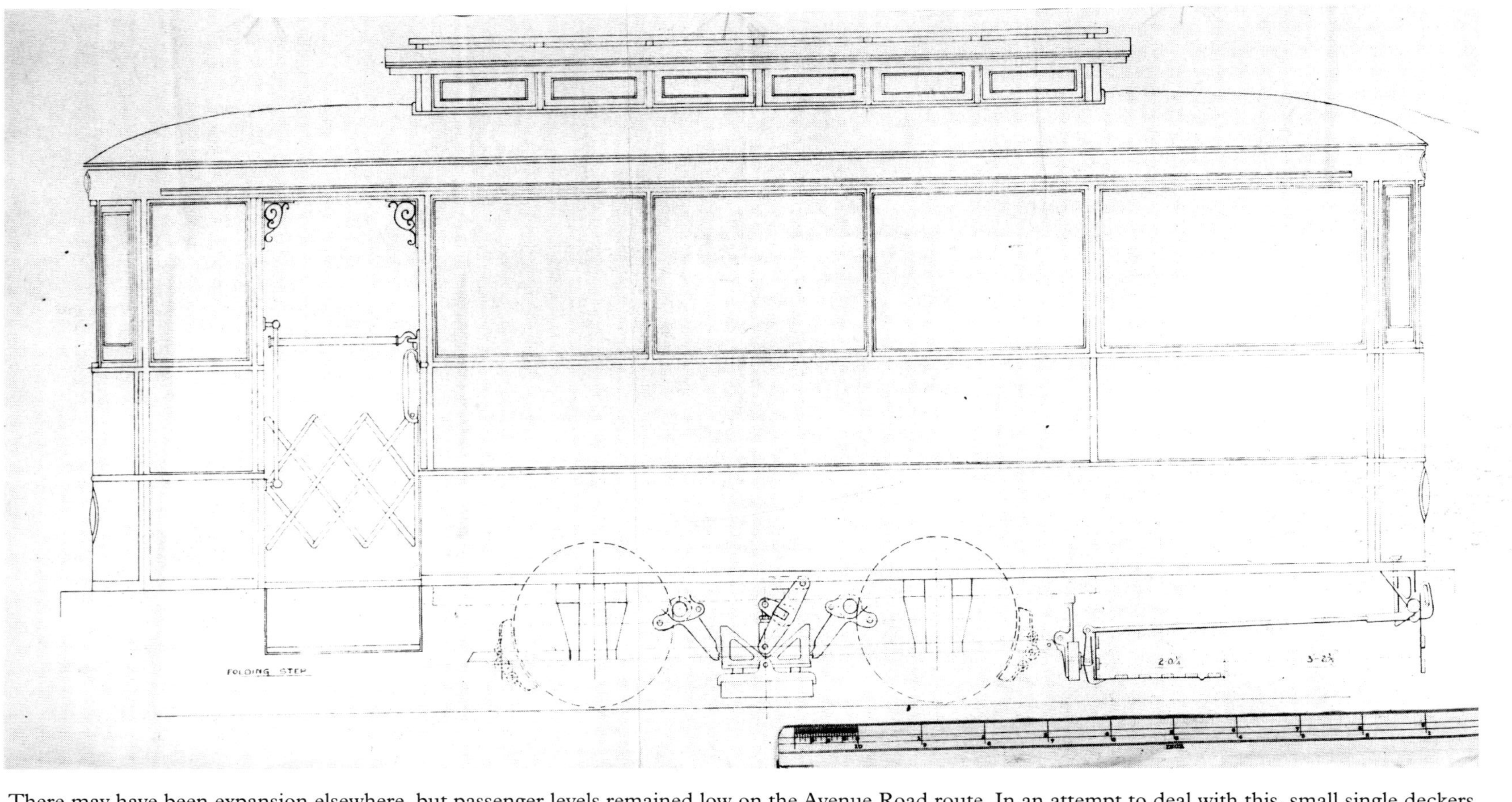

There may have been expansion elsewhere, but passenger levels remained low on the Avenue Road route. In an attempt to deal with this, small single deckers known as demi-cars were considered in 1908 and in 1917 one was purchased from Erith Corporation. It had just 20 seats and required only a driver, past whom passengers boarded via the front entrance. One lady is reputed to have refused the invitation to do this and to have gone round to the back instead, 'You've got this tram the wrong way round', she said! All to no avail, as the unions demanded a two-man crew, so the car was rarely used and was scrapped at an early date. *Charles Hall collection*

In 1915 the tracks were extended from Balby to Warmsworth to provide a service for miners at Edlington Main colliery. The terminus was on the main road to Conisbrough and Sheffield outside the *Cecil & Battie-Wrightson Arms* (this family owned nearby Cusworth Hall). The capacity of the power station was increased at the same time. This picture was taken not long after as the tram is still on the through service to Beckett Road, which ceased in 1917. Although it is wartime, a male conductor is working the duty. However, by 1917, seventy-five per cent of drivers were women and eighty-two men had left for military service. *David Packer collection*

The final wartime extension came in 1916 when a long route was completed out to Woodlands. The opening was delayed because the Post Office refused to move its telegraph poles. Car 30 of the short balcony class stands at the two-track terminus opposite the parade of shops, which has changed surprisingly little over the past eighty years. A lorry disappears into the distance, but children can still stand and stare curiously at the photographer in the middle of what became the A1.

The terminus was always described as Brodsworth, for although the village of that name was a mile or so sway, the colliery shared the same appellation. *Charles Hall collection*

After the war the department had ambitious plans for further routes out to more distant colliery villages at Armthorpe, Hatfield and Rossington. Legislation was prepared, but never submitted, and in 1922 the Corporation's first motor buses were purchased; services to Hatfield, Rossington and Skellow (another mining district) began towards the end of that year. However, it was too late to cancel an order for ten new trams, 38-47, which were the only ones in Doncaster to have fully enclosed drivers' cabs. They were delivered in 1920 and required an annex to the depot to house them. *Author's collection*

The original Warmsworth terminus was quickly found to be a hindrance to traffic on the main road to Sheffield, today's A630, and a short extension was authorised in 1916, though it was not built until 1919. 46 is pictured on the spur in Edlington Lane, just beside the local branch of the Co-op. The smart new livery has quickly disappeared under the usual enamelled metal advertisements, the agent for which was a London firm, J W Courtenay. Male crews became the rule again after the war; no new women were taken on and returning servicemen regained their jobs. *Author's collection*

The same scene, taken from the main road this time, and with Car 42 waiting to return to Doncaster. A special reversing spur in the overhead meant that the conductor did not have to swing the trolley. Some short workings still turned at Oswin Avenue. Traffic was not as high as had been expected, as private motor buses were able to carry miners all the way to Edlington; eventually, the Corporation had to set up its own service in competition. *Author's collection*

Meanwhile the shorter town routes continued as before. This view of Beckett Road terminus must have been taken after the war, as the foundation stones of the Methodist Church behind the railing to the right were not laid until 1913. The conductor is 'swinging the trolley' before the tram returns to the town centre, a necessary chore except at the Racecourse and Warmsworth terminals. *Author's collection*

LYONS
JELLY
CRYSTALS
HALK
DONCASTER.   W3.

Again, probably a post-war view because of the later livery style. The tram, one of the originals, is in surprisingly good condition, however, and is probably one of those fully reconditioned after years of wartime neglect. The dead-straight line of the body is particularly notable, as old trams often started to sag alarmingly. The car has been posed at the transport department's favourite spot for official views for many years after this, at the Racecourse, and is standing on the circular track behind the Grandstands. *Author's collection*

The tram track on the left of this 1920s view of the Great North Road at Woodlands was of a new type for Doncaster and fairly advanced for any town when it was laid in 1915-16. Leaving town, just before the bridge over the GC and Hull & Barnsley Joint Railway, the line moved from the street to a reservation along the side of the road, a position it maintained right up to Woodlands terminus. Railway-style track like this was cheaper to build and to maintain, and of course it had the great advantage of not impeding the growing number of motor vehicles. *Charles Hall collection*

In the early 1920s a scheme was proposed to ease the overcrowding caused by the single line along St Sepulchre Gate and to build an 'avoiding line' along Factory Lane and Trafford Street to North Bridge Road. In the event only the spur into Trafford Street was build, probably in 1922, and even this was not connected to the main line until a couple of years later. This picture is taken in Trafford Street looking towards French Gate and shows car 42 waiting to leave for Brodsworth. Bentley trams also used this spur.

Maurice O'Connor/copyright David Packer

This view shows the turnout from Trafford Street in the direction of Bentley and Brodsworth. It was put into use in 1924 after the Borough Surveyor had been instructed to install points so that trams could pull off the busy main road and reverse in the side street. Whereas the building on the left of the tram in the previous picture is still standing at the time of writing, those on the opposite side of the street have long ago been demolished to make way for the inner ring road, known as Trafford Way. This is Doncaster's last tram, number 47.
Charles Hall

After the First World War, motor bus competition grew rapidly. The problem was not so much the large companies such as Underwoods (today the East Midlands subsidiary of Stagecoach) with whom the Corporation could come to some formal agreement, but the small one-man firms, often known as 'pirates'. W E Goodyear licensed his bus for a service to Carcroft via Toll Bar in 1920. It was called Ruby after his daughter and had 14 seats. Small proprietors such as him often used their vehicles indiscriminately as lorries or buses, it just depended on the traffic which offered. Driver Reg Morrell is pictured at Carcroft.
Courtesy of Mrs R Roberts

By the 1920s Doncaster's trams were beginning to look dated and some, such as number 3, remained in original condition under their withdrawal. A policeman on point duty controls the traffic at Clock Corner, still in those days part of the London to Edinburgh trunk road. The view of Baxter Gate has not changed much, but the *Albany Hotel*, in the background, has disappeared. The Avenue Road tram route was replaced by a motor bus service to Wheatley Hills on 29 April 1925. However, within a month, the trams were brought back to supplement the buses at peak hours and even replaced them entirely when it was foggy. It is not known when the trams stopped finally. *Author's collection*

Possibly this is the same policeman on the same day. To modern eyes the traffic appears almost laughably light, but it was increasingly felt to be an issue in the inter-war period. And trams, however unjustly, were regarded by the motoring lobby as obstructive. The foreground of this picture shows French Gate, an area of central Doncaster which has changed beyond recognition.

Boots, the chemist, occupies an elegant shop opposite the *Angel & Royal Hotel*, the latter, of course, having been demolished to make way for the modern French Gate Centre. Boots shop too has been replaced by a newer building, but the other one with a bow window survives, though sadly without the window. *Author's collection*

Manoeuvring trams in and out of the Station Road terminus became more and more difficult, so about 1928 cars stopped using it and loaded in St Sepulchre Gate instead. This old tram did receive a top deck, but the extra weight of these often made the condition of the vehicle worse as time went by. Certainly, the platforms on this car have begun to sag noticeably. If the trams were to continue, a new fleet would have been required. All except the building on the extreme right of the picture were demolished and rebuilt in the inter-war years. The one immediately behind the tram became the *Nag's Head Hotel* and the one beyond is the site of the Co-op Bank today. *Author's collection*

Returning to Bentley, this fully paved loop on the approaches to the railway bridge was added about 1909, but the old line was left unimproved. Almost all this route was in the territory of Bentley Urban District Council and the West Riding and there was constant friction between them and the Corporation. In 1917 the Borough Surveyor complained about badly made roads with 'insufficiently pitched foundations' and a 'thin wearing crust', obvious problems here. In the end when the County decided in 1923 to reconstruct the road, Doncaster resolved to supplant the trams by trolleybuses rather than go to the expense of raising the track to the new level required. Only a year later it was decided to gradually replace all the trams. *Peter Tuffrey collection*

The first four trolleybuses were ordered from Garretts of Leiston in Suffolk, who were an early and small scale builder of these vehicles. Just as with motor-buses to this day, the chassis usually came from one builder and the bodywork from another, in this case Charles Roe of Leeds. All trolleybuses bought new or rebodied by Doncaster had Roe bodies. The first thirty one vehicles ordered were all broadly similar to number 1, with projecting cabs (the roofs leaked), a six-axle chassis (necessary because of contemporary axle-weight restrictions) and the projecting hood at the front to shield the ventilation louvre to the upper deck. This picture and the one overleaf may not have been taken in Doncaster at all, as they were taken by a Leeds photographer. The body frame was built of Burma teak, the bottom deck was panelled in steel and the top in mahogany. Number 1 acted as a driver training vehicle from March to August 1928 before the Bentley route was converted from tram to trolleybus, and then again for two years before its withdrawal in 1938. Available wiring on the Racecourse route was used for this purpose in 1928, and where the wiring was incomplete, a special contact called a skate was trailed in the tram rail to provide a return circuit. *Charles Hall collection*

Above is a side view of number 1 and below is the Karrier-Clough (later just Karrier) chassis used for subsequent pre-war deliveries. Unlike on tramcars, there is only a single motor and the controller is mounted under the floor and controlled by a foot pedal (one or two very early trolleybuses still had a hand operated controller, which must have been rather difficult to manage safely given that a steering wheel was also required!). The two rear axles acted rather like a railway bogie. Pneumatic brakes were fed with an air supply from a compressor. These were the first six-wheel trolleybuses by either Garretts or Karrier provided with pneumatic tyres. *Howard Turner collection/Tramway & Railway World*

These views of the lower and upper saloons show how light and pleasant the interior of these buses was, quite a contrast to the varnished woodwork of the old trams. The lower saloon does, however, retain a length of bench seating because this provided more room for standing passengers near the rear exit. There was space for 60 seated passengers on comfortable upholstered seats, again a rarity on trams anywhere then and certainly unheard of in Doncaster. The seats were covered in leather rather than the more usual moquette fabric. A sudden stop probably had lone passengers sliding from one end of the benches to the other! The floors were made of English oak and slatted, just as tram floors were. Each trolleybus cost just under £2,000. *Tramway & Railway World*

The first trolleybus service, to Bentley, was opened on 22 August 1928. The civic party made an opening run at 11.00 a.m. from the Mansion House in number 4 and are said to have passed tram 13 (appropriately) making the final tram trip to Bentley. The trolleybuses did not use Trafford Street as a terminus because they needed space to turn. So they simply crossed from one side of North Bridge Road to the other; the overhead wiring is just visible in this view. That was fine on a day when there wasn't much traffic, but it must have become increasingly difficult as the decades passed and the A1 got busier. *Charles Hall collection*

❖

Partly again to provide a turning facility and also to cover a wider area, the new trolleybuses did not stop at the New Village terminus, but were continued in a wide loop along Victoria Road and Askern Road. Buses ran round this in an anti-clockwise direction and thus required only a single set of wires, as on the former tram route here on Arksey Lane. Though the route length was longer, running time was reduced. The original plans also allowed for an extension further along the Askern Road as far as Toll Bar, but this was never built. *Charles Hall collection*

This postcard from the early 1930s shows three of the original pattern of trolleybus in St Sepulchre Gate. At this date there were two sets of wires going towards Clock Corner, the inner pair used by the Wheatley Hills (an extension of the former Avenue Road tram route) and Beckett Road services, the outer by buses heading for the Racecourse. The tram tracks, now disused, had been relayed in a new asphalt surface in 1926. Many of the old shops on the right hand side have been replaced by new premises in the latest art deco style. The *Nags Head Hotel*, above the sweet shop, has a very elegant horse's head carved on the frontage to complement its name. *Charles Hall collection*

The Racecourse conversion was done in two stages. On 16 January 1930 the Hyde Park route was turned over to trolleybuses and extended along Carr House Road to the Racecourse; the grassed central strip along here had originally been intended for a tramway extension, but that never materialised. At the same time the Racecourse trams were withdrawn and replaced by a temporary motor bus service. Two months later, on 20 March, trolleys took over. Thereafter a circular service was worked in both directions. Number 16, as it passes the Westminster Bank in High Street, shows how the new buses could join the traffic stream, assisted of course by the double 'track' (the Priory Place loop was abandoned). *Charles Hall collection*

Further out the Great North Road provides plenty of road space for the new trolleybuses and for the burgeoning number of motor cars. There is little sign of housing though, and it is obvious why this tram route only paid when there was a race meeting. The tracks have still not been lifted, a job which was nearly always deferred until road reconstruction became due. The other routes, all complete by 1931, were to Balby, Beckett Road, Hexthorpe and Wheatley Hills. *Tramways & Railway World*

This left only one tram route running, that to Brodsworth. Since it had been built later than the others and used trams which were only about ten years old, it made financial sense to utilise the assets until it became uneconomic to do so. This view of car 46 at one of the passing loops on the reserved track was therefore probably taken during the early 1930s. When the route did close, the last trams were sold to a scrap dealer for just £130. Four employees could not be found other jobs and were paid off. *P Henson/Charles Hall collection*

This tram is on the street track at the Doncaster end of the route. The railway bridge in the background carried, and still carries, a goods avoiding line allowing trains to/from Hull to divert around the town without going through the busy passenger station. This bridge was slightly lower than its twin to the right, which formerly spanned the Bentley tracks. Many of the old top covered cars were slightly too high for it and could not run to Brodsworth. So the newest cars were always used to Woodlands, even before the older cars were withdrawn. *Charles Hall*

This final picture of a Doncaster tram shows one of the 38-47 class running towards the town centre over Marsh Gate Bridge and an arm of the River Don, in full flood. No one seems too worried about getting their feet wet, however! The tram is being followed by a long distance coach, some of which were by then providing competition to the railways. This picture is dated May 1932, almost exactly three years before the last tram ran, on 8 June 1935. In this case Corporation motor-buses were used as tram replacements, not trolleybuses, which were seen as particularly advantageous on busy town routes with frequent stops and starts. *Author's collection*

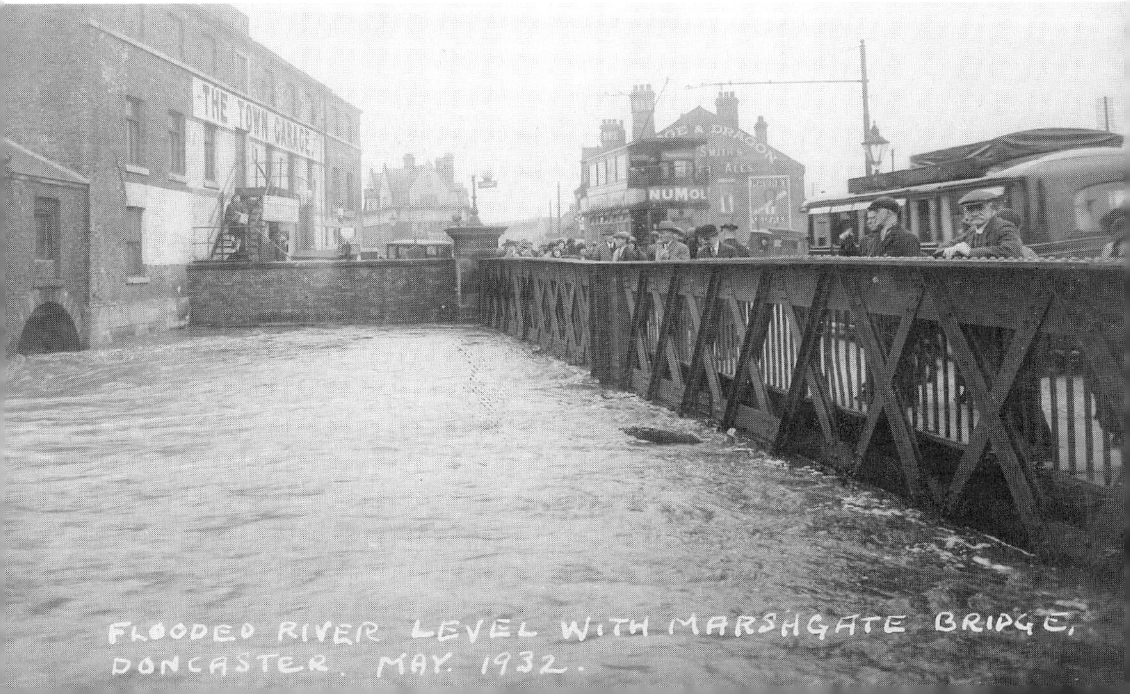

2:4Y. The Clock Corner. Doncaster.

There had been endless discussions in committee and on the council about diversionary tram routes in the town centre, but little apart from the Trafford Street stub had come of them. It was much easier to provide alternative routings for trolleybuses. Here number 11 passes Clock Corner along Baxtergate en route for Wheatley Hills or Beckett Road. Note that it has a variant livery with all maroon below the window level. Buses on these routes left via the former single track tram route, but they returned, as demonstrated by 23 on the second postcard, via a new loop along Silver Street and Cleveland Street, eventually joining the old 'Racecourse' loop along Printing Office Street. Just one set of wires was required, of course, and it made the best use of the narrow streets in the town centre. *Charles Hall collection*

Silver Street from Cleveland Street, Doncaster. "Empire View"

This picture is full of fascinating period detail. An ice cream seller drives his pony and trap past the bus, which is followed by a steam lorry. Number 16 has just reversed at the original Beckett Road terminus at Wentworth Road, a little beyond the former tram terminus. There was no room for a turning circle here, so buses had to reverse rather awkwardly using a triangle or wye in the wiring. The conductor is standing on the back platform because he had to supervise this operation to make sure that the trolleys stayed on the wires. *Charles Hall collection*

Number 14 displays the later livery without the cream panel below the waist rail. The growing amount and variety of motor traffic along St Sepulchre Gate West also illustrates the advantage the more flexible trolleybuses had over trams which had mostly been confined to single tracks. When tramway retention was still a live issue, reconstruction with double lines was soon seen to be a minimum requirement, though further extensions, such as the later trolleybus line to Wheatley Hills, would probably also have been necessary. All this was too costly for Doncaster, especially as the debt on the original tramway was not fully paid off. So conversion to trolleybuses was almost certainly the right decision at the time.

Charles Hall collection

Hallgate from South Parade, Doncaster.　"Empire View" 01·215

A 'red' bus runs out on the Racecourse circle along Hall Gate and South Parade. It is passing the Gaumont Picture Palace, a splendid period building which is today one of the fairly rare town centre cinemas anywhere to be still serving its original purpose, now under the Odeon banner. Certainly until a decade ago it could still double as a theatre for the occasional event such as a pantomime. One of the earliest sets of traffic lights in the town was installed here. At off-peak times they were set to flash on yellow so as not to hold vehicles up when nothing was coming the other way. Locals christened the lights 'blinking 'orace'. *Charles Hall collection*

72

In 1934 Karrier produced a new chassis which was bodied by Roe in a more modern style as number 32 in the Doncaster fleet. There was still a vestigial bonnet, but the top deck was fully extended over the cab. Oddly, this did not give space for any extra seats. The design owed quite a lot to the technical input of Mr T Potts, the Manager since 1920, and the bus was exhibited at the Commercial Motor Show of that year. This official view has been posed outside the electricity works in Greyfriars Road. This bus remained a 'one-off', and later deliveries had a flat front without the angular appearance of this one. *Charles Hall collection*

Number 18 leads a line up of nine of the original fleet to show off the workmanship of the body builders, Charles Roe of Leeds. A small girl, seeing the trolley booms appearing to hang on the wires, called these 'monkey buses'. Trams required only a single overhead wire as current could be returned via the steel rails, but trolleybuses needed both a positive and a negative wire. The tramway overhead support poles were re-used in 'light duty' locations, but on curves etc. had to be replaced by heavier ones. The spider's web of wires, especially at junctions, could sometimes be rather oppressive. Neither was much of a problem in Doncaster; much of the wiring was 'single line' and junctions were few and simple. Too simple, in fact, for in quite a few cases trolleybuses had to have their booms detached whilst they ran over a 'dead' section by gravity; not a practice which the Health & Safety Executive would be likely to approve today! *Charles Hall collection*

Trolleybus 54 dates from June 1939 and the sports car is in period, but the saloon in the background and the post-1948 fleet number of 354 give the game away. The actual date is October 1954. First of the buildings on the left is 1 Marsh Gate, a much older building which had been the town dispensary and then formed the first offices for the transport department after it was split from the electricity department in 1920. Next to it is an overflow tram shed which was built in the same year to house the expanding fleet. Beyond that again is the electric power station of 1899. The main tram and later trolleybus depot was on the opposite side of the road. *David Packer*

365 was one of no less than twenty new trolleybuses which joined the fleet in 1939. It was one of two delivered in August and was followed by three more in September, when war was declared, after which such peacetime vehicles became unobtainable. All buses from (3)33 onwards were of this basic design with an unobstructed and slightly swept back front end, giving them a suitably 1930s streamlined look. The three white band livery had been introduced for experimental bus (3)32 and suited these handsome vehicles well. 365 is standing in West Laithe Gate, which was the terminus for buses to Hexthorpe and Balby. *David Packer*

The Second World War marked another turning point. By 1940 some of the oldest trolleybuses were getting beyond redemption and the Corporation tried and failed to buy six new ones. In 1943 the Ministry of War Transport gave permission to buy three. Just as clothing and furniture was produced to utility standards, so were public transport vehicles. A standard W-type chassis was produced and 370 was the second bus delivered. Only two firms were allowed to build the bodies, so the Corporation had to desert Roe's in favour of Park Royal. Though some repair work had been done and the grey livery replaced by red and white, the angular utility style is obvious in this picture, taken in Greyfriars Road in 1957. *David Packer*

This is 370 again, pictured on a short length of St Sepulchre Gate that had no less than four pairs of overhead wires. Those alongside the pavement were added later for Bentley route buses travelling from the depot (against the traffic flow) or back again, which they did by using wires along Factory Lane and Trafford Street, the planned but never completed tramway loop. The shopping scene has changed a lot since the mid-1950s. Blakes, nearest the camera, and Bells the Jewellers are both local firms, whilst Burtons advertises itself as 'The Fifty Shilling Tailors'. *David Packer*

All the wartime buses were later provided with modern Roe bodies, like 375, one of the final six new vehicles bought, and shown standing here in Greyfriars Road outside the electricity generating station. There were six extra seats, which obviously made the vehicles more economical to operate. This body style was accompanied by the introduction of a new standard livery of crimson lake (rather brighter than maroon) with a single white band. This is a very late view, taken in February 1963. *David Parker*

By the early 1950s the remaining three axle buses were due for replacement. It was decided to standardise on two axle vehicles, which were more economical to run. At the time, however, the long-term future of the trolleybuses was in some doubt, so six second-hand vehicles were purchased from Darlington for a total of £17,433. They were only three years old, as Darlington too had been unsure over whether or not to keep its trolleys, and fairly quickly decided not to do so. Their number 68, which became Doncaster 378, is pictured on Low Flags, Darlington, during its brief stay in that town. 378-383 had chassis supplied by British United Traction (BUT) and bodies by the East Lancashire Company, both unique in the Doncaster fleet. *David Packer*

At first the Darlington buses kept the same style of livery with white window surrounds. 380, pictured, and 378 were later repainted in the standard three-band colour scheme and eventually received the single-band version. 380 is pictured in 1957, a couple of years before its service in Doncaster came to an end, outside the Astra cinema on Beckett Road. Unlike the trams, the trolleybus services had numbers. Bentley was 1, Hexthorpe, Wheatley, Beckett Road and Racecourse/Hyde Park were 3-6, and Balby was 10. *David Packer*

When withdrawn from service in 1959, these buses were only ten years old, which for an electric vehicle is quite new. So they sold on yet again, to Bradford, whose General Manager, Chaceley Humpidge, was making a determined effort to keep trolley services going by purchasing and modernising second-hand buses. By that time, no one was building new ones. So 378-83 were transferred to West Yorkshire in January 1960, 378 for spares only. The others were rebuilt with new front entrance East Lancashire bodies and renumbered 831-835. Here 835 is running on route 37, which served the village of Clayton between 1926 and 1971. Bradford buses were painted a rather pleasant shade of light blue. Several buses, including ex-Doncaster 382/3, have survived into preservation. *Michael Faulkner*

The long-serving Manager, Mr T Potts, retired in 1953 and was succeeded by Mr T Bamford, who came from Maidstone Corporation. He was far less of a workaholic and is said to have liked his golf! In 1949 Potts had considered abandoning the trolleybuses, though he later agreed to buy 40 new ones, but only if they had three-axles. In 1953 Bamford recommended withdrawing trolleys from Hexthorpe and Beckett Road, but the Committee voted for higher capacity trolleybuses instead. Like Bradford, however, fleet renewal took place through purchases from the many systems that were dispensing with electric transport at this period. One reason for this was that with the nationalisation of electricity supply, municipalities ceased to have an interest in maintaining a load on their generating stations and, instead, found themselves paying high rates for their current. Southend-on-Sea 130-138, utility vehicles dating from 1945-46, were bought in 1954, the same year that the sea-side town's last route, from Victoria Circus to Boulevard, was closed. This is 133 in its home town. *Dennis Gill*

Ex-Southend 135 is now Doncaster 389 and is in service on the Hexthorpe route in 1955. It has a Park Royal utility body. Balby buses also used West Laithe Gate, which formed a useful loop for turning trolleybuses. However the old three-axle bus behind is out of service as it has its trolleys tied down. The Balby stop was just in front of the Hexthorpe one. *David Packer*

Between 1956 and 1959 all the ex-Southend buses were given new Roe bodies of the standard Doncaster pattern. By the late 1950s the eventual closure of the trolleybus system was envisaged, so the new bodies were built to be usable on motor buses. All were transferred to new Leyland chassis after only a few years service. 391 is at the same stop as 389, seven years later, and just before the Balby service was converted to motor-bus operation. The Cake Shop is in the ground floor of the King's Arcade, which provided space for a number of shops and, on the upper floors, the Doncaster Registry Office before it moved to more sylvan surroundings at Elmfield Park. *David Packer*

In 1955 six vehicles came from much nearer home, from the fleet of the Mexborough & Swinton Traction Company, which was one of the relatively few company-operated trolleybus systems in the country. Because of low bridges on their route they used single-deck buses, and this view shows number 2 still with its Brush-built body in the depot at Doncaster. None of the buses were used as single-deckers, however, but received one of the usual Roe double-deck bodies before re-entering service. *Geoff Warnes*

The new double-deck bodies were fitted to all the ex-Mexborough buses in the same year they were bought. 394, the first to be dealt with, has been photographed on 18 September 1955 and is obviously fresh out of the paintshop. It may even have been photographed at Roe's works in Leeds, as this is not a recognisable Doncaster scene. The bus must have looked very smart in its bright red paintwork relieved with white. This body too was later transferred to a motor-bus, in his case Leyland PD2/1 188.

David Packer

The penultimate purchase was two 1944 chassis from Pontypridd Urban District Council in South Wales. As usual, Roe supplied new bodies. Because older buses had by now been withdrawn, the pair received previously used numbers, becoming 351/2. The former is seen on Carr House Lane, just past the Racecourse on its way back to town via Hyde Park. *David Packer*

The very last additions were two more ex-Mexborough buses, 353/354. 18, which became 354, arrived without its body, which was kept as a store in Rawmarsh depot. 353 stands inside Greyfriars depot beside 374. There are still traces of tram rail in the floor. Motorbuses had been garaged at the former aerodrome since their inception, and an extension of the wiring to this site had been planned. The 1937-built bus garage at Leicester Avenue, Intake, actually had the words 'Trolley Vehicle Entrance' carved into the lintel of one doorway. However, the necessary extension was not constructed due to the outbreak of war in 1939, and Ministry permission was again refused in 1949, so the trolleys always remained at Greyfriars Road. By this time, February 1963, the depot was almost empty. *David Packer*

Two trolleybus 'clippies', with Mary Martin (later Mrs House) on the right, pose in the centre of town. Doncaster began using women again as conductresses on single-deck motor-buses in the early 1920s, but did not believe that trolleybuses were women's work, especially due to the need to manhandle the trolley booms on occasion. The Second World War changed all that, and the first girls were employed from August 1941. Their equipment includes a leather bag for the cash and heavy 'Ultimate' ticket machines. The latter issued pre-printed tickets at varying values and in different colours and only replaced traditional punches and racks in 1951. *Courtesy of Mrs M House*

There were six trolleybus routes and Bentley was the first both numerically and historically. This is a nice pose of three-axle bus 353 in Greyfriars Road outside the power station and the post-First World War tram shed. This was always known as the 'Village' depot, perhaps because it was used by Bentley buses. 353 has obviously just come off service. The driver has already gone off for his break and the conductor is just stepping off the back platform. Rear-entrance crew-operated buses seem a very distant memory, though oddly some of the most modern transport systems are reintroducing conductors today. In Sheffield, ticket issuing machines were an abject failure on Supertram and the system only took off when real people started selling the tickets. *David Packer*

This picture was taken in the late 1980s, long after the trolleybuses had disappeared, but it is still history. This back street was once part of French Gate, the route which the trams and most of the trolleys had taken to and from their depot. The concrete structure above and to the right, since demolished, was attached to the North Bridge in the late 1920s to provide a turning point for buses coming in from the north of the town. On 1 April 1974 Doncaster Corporation Transport lost its independence and became a part of the county-wide South Yorkshire Transport, the operator of Dennis Dominator 2260, seen here. Some things don't change though, as Bentley buses still followed much the same route as their predecessors. *The author*

A picture taken above and thirty years previously to the previous photograph shows 381 in its distinctive Darlington-style livery at the Bentley terminus. These desolate-looking concrete shelters were also used by motor-bus passengers catching services going out to the north of the town. The structure was demolished a number of years ago as part of a revamp designed to keep the North Bridge serviceable for a few more years until the present St George's Bridge was opened in 2001. *David Packer*

Many of the pre-war buses survived well into the post-war period, and though this photo is dated 1954, it could just as easily have been taken anytime within the previous twenty years. Once Bentley trolleys had come round Trafford Street from the depot, or had swung precariously across the A1 from their inbound stop, they picked up passengers from outside the Brown Cow public house. Rather conveniently for patrons, the pub has a Gents situated right next door! Rain, steam trains running up the East Coast Main Line, and the local mining industry combine to make this a somewhat drab scene. *David Packer*

A busy scene with three buses nose-to-tail on North Bridge Road. This is one of Doncaster's few gradients! The motor bus may belong to the Yorkshire Traction Company, which ran in from Barnsley via this route. 390 is operating the Bentley service and the pre-war three-axle trolleybus behind is a Special. In those days, and certainly before and during the war, cyclists rather than motorists probably provided public transport's major competition, especially in a flat area like this. *Geoff Warnes*

Ex-Darlington 381 has crossed the North Bridge and is just leaving the Mill Bridge and passing the *Three Horse Shoes* pub. This busy road is the A1, though the Bentley route turned off it to the A19 a 100 yards or so further on. 381 is being tailed by a extremely impressive Wolsley saloon! Mind you, at 120hp, these particular trolleys had more power than most vehicles on the road. They had markedly better acceleration than any of the other buses in the fleet. *Geoff Warnes*

Just beyond the *Three Horse Shoes* the Bentley wires went under the right hand of the two railway bridges carrying the goods avoiding line. Passengers were evidently regaled with the exhortation that 'GUINNESS IS GOOD FOR YOU'! The storage yards on the far side were associated with a quite separate railway, the former Hull & Barnsley/Great Central Joint. Planned as a passenger terminus, the York Road station never saw anything but freight trains.

The bus, one of the old three-axle type, is about to cross the Bentley flood arches, a sort of low bridge built to take account of the likelihood of flooding in this area. Even today, there is little building on the far side of the A19 here. *Geoff Warnes*

FOR YOU

These four snapshots were all taken by Rod Bramley and illustrate some of the peculiar local features of the overhead wiring in Doncaster.

In the first view, 375 is pictured in Greyfriars Road beside the former municipal power station. Its trolleys are on the last remaining section of 'double-single' wiring which formerly stretched from here to French Gate. The centre wire was used for travel in both directions, the outer wires in one direction only. The assumption was presumably that buses would all be running into or off service at similar times and so the stretch could be effectively one-way. Quite what the advantage over a simple set of double wires was is hard to see. By this date, 1963, Greyfriars Road was no longer used at all, so the wires are 'tied off' behind the bus.
Rod Bramley

In the second shot, 373 has reversed out from the depot in front of 375. To move forward to take up service (on the Racecourse route) the trolleys have to be re-poled.
Rod Bramley

Then 369 is shown under the triple set of running wires in St Sepulchre Gate. Because there were no overhead junctions in the centre, if a bus had arrived on one set of wires and needed to depart on another, it had again to be re-poled. Each bus was equipped with two bamboo poles for this purpose. At least on the old three-axle trolleybuses, the poles were stowed along the length of the vehicle through a hole in the rear of the bus. Though if a conductor needed a pole again shortly, he would wedge it on the rear platform, sticking up and outwards at 45°. *Rod Bramley*

Finally, there is a view taken looking down Highfield Road towards Wheatley Hills on 24 February 1963. Trolleybuses had been replaced by motor buses on this section two months earlier and most of the overhead had been removed, but the Doncaster Omnibus & Light Railway Society (DO&LRS), an enthusiast group, have persuaded the driver to reverse back on the remaining bit. What the picture does show is how heavy and unwieldy trolleybus wiring was at junctions. Overhead 'points' called frogs were fitted, and all the weight of ironmongery required extra span wires to support it. One can see why the DCT preferred to avoid junctions in the town centre.

Rod Bramley

Buses on route 3 came into the town centre via St Sepulchre Gate and then used the left hand set of overhead wires here to turn left into West Laithe Gate. The right hand pair were for buses coming from Hyde Park and towards the Racecourse. This postcard gives a good impression of how neat and unobtrusive trolleybus wiring could be. The job of overhead linesman was a skilled one. The wires had to be carefully pulled off for the curves so that the trolley booms went round smoothly. The booms, like those on trams, were spring loaded to keep them pressed up to the wires; if they came off, they sprang up with some force and could easily damage the overhead. *Charles Hall collection*

The street scene has been irrevocably changed by the great increase in motor traffic since the 1950s. Hexthorpe trolleys left the centre via St Sepulchre Gate, which at that time was a through road as far as this point, where it joined Cleveland Street. This fascinating view can be compared to Edwardian postcards of the trams, in which the YMCA building on the right also figures prominently. Behind it is a row of terrace houses, and both were demolished years ago to make way for the dual carriageway along Cleveland Way. This was the junction between the Hexthorpe and Balby trolleybus routes and some of the intricate wiring needed at such points is in evidence above 387, which is just turning on to the Hexthorpe wires. *David Packer*

The street in the background was split a long time ago by Clevland Way and not much remains now of the old properties on St Sepulchre Gate West. The school on the left has gone too, only the church and the ramp up to St James's Bridge remain. Trolleybus wiring was the same as that for the trams in that the voltage had to be boosted every half mile or so by feeder cables. These ran in underground conduits, and there is no reason why the old tram ones could not have been reused. Then the cable was taken up the overhead support pole and the current fed into the overhead wires themselves. A close examination will show that 391 is just passing under a feeder. *David Packer*

Bridge Terrace, on the far side of the bridge, was built for railway workers in the adjacent Plant Works. Densely packed housing like this was always good territory for either trams or trolleybuses, both of which required a fairly dense population and high ridership per mile to justify the investment in fixed equipment. This is why several of the Doncaster tram routes, such as the Avenue Road and Racecourse lines, never paid. 387, one of the ex-Southend buses, is disappearing back towards the town in the background and 374, one of the last new trolleys supplied to Doncaster in 1945, is travelling 'down', to make appropriate use of railway parlance. The houses here were long ago replaced by commercial premises.

Philip Robinson/Howard Turner collection

Hexthorpe is an area of the town which has changed surprisingly little over the decades. Presumably the outside toilet on the end of the first house was no longer serving its original purpose, even in 1961, but the terraces themselves still provide decent homes, forty years on. 388 was pictured on 26 March 1961, almost exactly a year before the trolleybus service was withdrawn. The bus itself was withdrawn in September 1962 and the chassis was sold for scrap. *Rod Bramley*

A fairly desolate scene as an ex-Southend bus approaches Hexthorpe terminus on 11 March 1962, less than a week before the closure of this route on 17 March. Trolleybuses had limited manoeuvrability, but at least they could pass parked vehicles, like this Austin saloon. The old limestone wall on the far side of the street is a reminder of Hexthorpe's rural past. *David Packer*

A couple of months earlier Howard Turner photographed 396 on a misty January day. The bus has swung round the loop from the previous picture, past the entrance to Hexthorpe Flatts in the background, and is 'laying over' here to allow the crew their rest time before returning to town. They will pick up passengers again at the shelter a bit further along the pavement. 396 was one of the former Mexborough single-deckers and would be withdrawn on the last day of 1962. Its body was then refitted to Leyland motor-bus 93, which dated originally from 1947 and was only four years newer than 396 itself. *Howard Turner*

Route 4 was unique in that it originally replaced a motor-bus route, not a tramway. The reason for this was that the Avenue Road trams were first replaced by motor-buses to Wheatley Hills in 1925-26 and then, in accordance with the Manager's preference for trolleybuses on urban routes, themselves superseded in 1931. There are many reminders of tramway days in this 1962 shot of the town terminus. The two buses are standing beside Hodgeson & Hepworth's store, one of the three firms who had operated the horse buses displaced by the trams. To the right is the old Co-op building, in front of which is Station Road. Right in the rear is West Laithe Gate, never used by trams but always a trolleybus terminus. *David Packer*

The ex-Darlington buses were the only second-hand purchases to run until withdrawal with their former owner's bodywork. This was because they were almost new when bought. 392 and another bus are swinging round the sharp bend between Kings Road and Thorne Road. The latter remains one of the main routes out of town and passes close to Doncaster Royal Infirmary. The Avenue Road trams had also used Kings Road and Thorne Road, but had not gone very far along it. Wheatley Hills included both council housing and private developments built after the tramway was opened, and it was to serve them that first motor-buses and then trolleybuses were extended out to the *Wheatley Hotel*. *David Clarke*

94

390, ex-Southend 137, is pictured in October 1954, just a few months after its transfer from the Essex resort. It will retain its utility body for a further four years. The location is the *Wheatley Hotel* (behind the bus) at the junction of Thorne Road and Barnby Dun Road. This was the original 1931 terminus for the trolleybus route. The electric lighting department have started installing concrete lamp standards to replace the earlier streetlights, which were often carried on the poles for the overhead; a saving for one municipal department and an income for the other.

David Packer

Four years later, on 14 October 1958, Doncaster's last trolleybus route extension took the wires a short way further out along Thorne Road to Sandall Park. This was not a housing estate, but a public park with a boating lake and other attractions. 385 stands at the new terminus, near the end of Sandall Park Road. A paved turning circle, which is still there, was specially built on the far side of the main road. This bus was out of service for most of 1958 being reconstructed by Roe, who removed the old utility body and replaced it with one of the standard 'rebuild' type. It came back into service on 1 December. *David Packer*

❖

Service 5 buses to Beckett Road started in St Sepulchre Gate just in front of the Wheatley Hills stop. A pair of utility vehicles stand awaiting departure at quite an early date. The town centre Co-op store remains at the top end of Station Road, Hodgson & Hepworth's is still open and Willows the 'modern outfitter' is evidently finding a market for his breeches. 384 was the first second-hand trolley acquired from Southend and was the only one to have a body built by Brush. A handful of tram top covers was the only other example of this firm's workmanship in the Doncaster electric fleet. *R Priestley*

Two interesting views of buses passing through the Market Place, in this case on the Beckett Road service. In the lower view 369 is followed by another bus round the corner of the Market Hall, out of sight on the left. The close-up shows 397 at the same point. As already mentioned, trolleybuses only needed to go through Baxtergate and the Markets in one direction, as they returned via Silver Street. The extra set of wires is therefore not for the other direction, but is part of a revised arrangement for access to the depot. The former tram/trolleybus exit via French Gate was dewired some time between 1957 and 1961, and all buses then entered and left via High Fisher Gate, and this is the place where that wiring, which was installed about 1930, began. It is a warm but windy day in September 1961 and 397's driver is in shirt sleeves, a special relaxation of uniform regulations permitted on hot days. All the industrial buildings and chimneys in the background have long disappeared, mostly to be replaced by yet more new roads. *David Packer*

In an earlier view, one of the utility buses is passing between the Corn Exchange (built in 1873 and well restored in 1997 after fire damage) and the stalls which fill every bit of open space. Doncaster first became a Borough with the right to hold a market in 1194, and this has remained an important part of the town's commercial life right up until the present day. So much has changed though. The hangers for a set of trolleybus wires going across at a right angle can be seen at the top of the photograph. These were for a loop line around the far side of the Market Hall intended to keep trolleybuses out of the town centre during race meetings, but in practice motor-buses were usually substituted on the Beckett Road and Wheatley services. *Author's collection*

388 on a rainy day in Nether Hall Road, just about to turn into Broxholme Lane. The other bus is probably on the Wheatley route, which continued straight along at this point. This is quite a late view as both buses are in the final 'single band' livery. Like so many other local products, Barnsley Brewery's Oakwell Ales are no longer available. Though Barnsley Bitter has become available again, and very good it is too! The rather imposing church in the background is not an Anglican edifice, as it might appear, but an uncharacteristically fancy Methodist chapel. It still stands, though it no longer serves as a church and has been adapted as part of a flats complex called Concorde Mews. *David Packer*

This pair of photographs is not quite what it seems, but it does illustrate one of the problems with trolleybus operation. The location is Holmes Market, a short street linking Broxholme Lane and Beckett Road. This particular view has not changed much. At first sight, this appears to show a bus which has failed in service being overtaken by another. The only way this could be done, except in the special case where an extra set of wires was provided, was by hauling down the trolley booms on one bus and letting the other one pass. This would be what happened in the case of a mechanical failure or an accident. However, the bus in the lead, advertising the long-gone cleaning product 'Wimzo', is 375. It is on hire to the DO&LRS for a special tour on 24 February 1963. 393, coming up behind, is in public service and needs to overtake. So one of the enthusiasts gets out and does the honours (usually the conductor's job of course). *David Packer*

The Beckett Road route was extended twice. First from Wentworth Road to the bottom end of the Parkway in April 1941 and finally from here to the top end of Beckett Road on 17 February 1958. The metal-clad council-built housing on the estate is typical of the period, as is the concrete road surface. The road here forms a loop, ideal for trolleybuses, and an ex-Mexborough bus is seen making its way round in August 1962. *David Packer*

387 has arrived at the new Beckett Road terminus, which was used only between 1958 and 1963. Like most contemporary housing estates, the district was provided with a parade of shops. Even then, it doesn't appear very prosperous, and has now been demolished and replaced by a group of bungalows. The Riley does look a rather superior mode of conveyance though! *David Packer*

On their return to the town centre Beckett Road buses reached their terminus via Printing Office Street, which had formerly been the site of the Racecourse tramway loop. By 1954, when this picture was taken, the old Co-op shop at the end of Station Road had been replaced by the new department store on the right; it is now a branch of the T J Hughes chain. The Central Hall, above the shops to the left, was leased as a town centre office and crew rest room from 1924 to about 1943. 348 was one of the pre-war three-axle trolleys and was the last of the 1938 delivery to be withdrawn, in 1955. *David Packer*

398 was the last bus to be numbered 'in series', so it was the ninety-eighth trolleybus in the fleet. It is standing at the front of the Co-op store at the St Sepulchre Gate terminus for buses going in the Hyde Park direction on the Racecourse circular. Perhaps the opportunity given by the building of the new shop was used to construct a lay-by for the buses; otherwise, except for Bentley route, this was a luxury conspicuous by its absence in the narrow central streets. The Hyde Park/Racecourse route was numbered 6. *David Packer*

Buses travelling direct to the Racecourse left from St Sepulchre Gate, using the outer pair of wires; the inner pair were those used by Bentley buses on depot trips. All this mixed commercial property was to be swept away when the French Gate Centre was constructed. Ex-Darlington vehicles, like 378, always looked slightly different, even when repainted in the standard livery. This was because they alone retained their original non-standard bodies which had a slightly deeper band above the windows in which were three ventilators. *David Packer*

The next long street beyond Spring Gardens was Catherine Street. 397 has been photographed in Catherine Street quite late in the life of the route, on 4 March 1961. Like Hexthorpe, Hyde Park was a district of close-packed terrace houses built during the nineteenth century industrial expansion of the town. The 1899 Light Railway Order authorised a tramway only to the far end of Catherine Street, the Carr House Road part being an afterthought covered by the 1902 Order. *Lyndon Rowe*

These pictures show Spring Gardens, a street which ran between St Sepulchre Gate and
Waterdale. Only the lower section, shown above, still has this name, but all the old
property behind the parked buses was knocked down years ago; nothing was built in its
place. 375, 382 and 391 are Racecourse specials, which on race days ran only via Hyde
Park; the other side of the circle was suspended. Until 1934 racegoers had been herded
on to the direct buses at a premium fare, but residents could travel via Hyde Park at
ordinary fares; that was until some helpful citizen told the visitors! The other half of the
street, shown below, was renamed College Road. The building site on the left has been
cleared for the construction of the South Bus Station, which, in the first decade of the
twenty-first century, is itself to be replaced by a modern Interchange. The old baths on
Waterdale are still is use, however. The trolleybus is returning from Hyde Park. Wiring on
the nearer side of the road has already been dismantled, because for the last few months
trolleys only ran this way round the route; the opposite 'circle' was already the preserve
of motor buses. *Philip Robinson/Howard Turner collection*

102

376 is outward bound to the Racecourse via High Street. In 1963 the National Provincial and Westminster Banks had evidently still not merged, as the imposing bank premises still belong to the latter concern. The banking hall inside is one of Doncaster's finest interiors, and to the bank's credit it has not been subdivided by screens or false ceilings. The National Westminster itself is now part of a larger group, of course. The same process of 'bigger is better' has affected local transport too, where municipal ownership and operation of buses and trams has become a part of history and most bus services are run by one of three or four major companies. The majority of South Yorkshire buses are now owned by First Bus. *David Packer*

377 is on the roundabout at the end of Bennetthorpe with some of the Racecourse buildings in the background. One of the reasons why trolleybuses were eventually abandoned was that whenever the street layout was altered, the wiring had to be modified. In this case, when the roundabout was built about 1959, eighteen new poles were planted, the wiring was changed and the trolleys continued to run. But it was felt that as further streets were rebuilt, the need to move the poles and wires would be a hindrance. *David Packer*

375 has just turned the corner into Carr House Lane, going from the Racecourse towards Hyde Park. This section of road never had a tram track, so the circular route was purely a trolleybus operation. It proved to be a very efficient way of moving the vast crowds to and from the races, especially pre-war, when most racegoers either used public transport or walked. *David Packer*

The Balby route was numbered 10 and it was the last trolleybus route to be opened, in 1931. This is a fairly early picture of a bus in 1954 on its way from the depot to enter service. Greyfriars Road was in the background to the right and on the left is the North Bridge. 392 is just passing the *Volunteer Inn*, French Gate, quite a rustic looking building, long gone now of course. 392 was the last of the ex-Southend utility vehicles and would not be rebodied for a further four years. *Geoff Warnes*

Two years later 391 was photographed at the outer terminus, Barrel Lane. The route was extended out here in July 1942, though the original plan in 1930 had been to run the wires right out to Edlington. There was plenty of space for a turning circle off the main A630 to Sheffield and the trees make it look quite rural. The driver is having five minutes in the fresh air. It was always said that a conductor's life was a more healthy one, as he got plenty of exercise, whereas drivers were cooped up in a cab and must have suffered increasingly from stress as traffic levels built up. *Howard Turner*

It is obviously a hot summer's day (remember them?) as 350 demonstrates the way its half-drop windows provide ample ventilation on both decks of the older vehicles. It too is standing at Barrel Lane. Notice the clearly displayed route number 10 and how it is concealed in the previous photograph. This is because late in the life of the system route numbers were officially discontinued for Corporation services, though of course nobody was going to spend money on new blinds. *Howard Turner*

This illustrates an interesting episode in South Yorkshire's transport history. The only other trolleybuses in the county ran in the Rotherham area. Both the Mexborough Company and the Corporation had fleets entirely made up of single deckers. However, in 1955 Rotherham Corporation decided that the higher capacity of double deck vehicles would be desirable. Before coming to a final decision they wanted to check clearances using a double deck trolleybus. For this purpose, Doncaster Corporation loaned 362, an old three-axle bus. It was taken across to Rotherham on 19 June 1955. It ran under its own power to Balby and was then towed along the A630 by DCT breakdown truck 362 until it reached the Rotherham wires at Thrybergh. The pair are shown there, together with a Rotherham tower wagon. Finally, 362 is shown ready to test the clearances inside the Rotherham depot, at Parkgate. Geoff Warnes followed the Rotherham part of the journey on his bicycle and on arriving at Parkgate was invited in by the Manager to take some official pictures; nobody had remembered to arrange a photographer to record this important event! This was not the first time that a Doncaster trolleybus had run under 'foreign' wires. In 1930-31 two buses were used as Karrier demonstrators in four towns, Nottingham, Mexborough, Johannesburg and York. Rotherham Corporation fitted twenty trolleybuses with double-deck bodies after 1955 and some of them ran until 1965. *Geoff Warnes*

In the end, Doncaster's trolleybuses were all withdrawn two years before Rotherham's. The decision was taken in October 1962 and the changeover was very rapid. The principal reasons were the cost of wiring and major changes to the street network, which threatened the ability to recoup capital expenditure over a long enough period. Trolleys were being abandoned everywhere, making the provision of spare parts and replacements increasingly difficult. This bus is about to pass the DO&LRS tour on 24 February 1963 at Holmes Market and is on a service to Clay Lane, probably an extension of the former Wheatley Hills trolleybus route. It was, of course, much easier to extend diesel buses as the town grew than it was electric ones. *Philip Robinson/Howard Turner collection*

The tour trolleybus passes motor-bus 171, which is standing at the Wheatley Hills stop in St Sepulchre Gate. Just under a year before trolleybus 352(2) had been withdrawn and its body passed to 171, which was a new Daimler vehicle. The main difference was the replacement of the full cab front with the traditional half cab design used for the front-engined motor-buses of the day. A total of nineteen trolleybus bodies were re-used in this way. One of these, 188, survived into the ownership of South Yorkshire PTE and is still extant and in Doncaster livery; in mid-2002 it was in the First Mainline workshops in Rotherham being restored to full operating condition for private hire duties. *Philip Robinson/Howard Turner collection*

The DO&LRS had a further tour on 13 December 1963, one day before the final close-down of the trolleybus system. Here is a group of enthusiasts posed in front of 377 at the depot. This bus had been the last one on the Racecourse service, exactly two months earlier. As is the way of such things, the gathering is more or less exclusively male, though the number of women involved at places such as the National Tramway Museum and at Sandtoft is growing all the time. After all transport operation itself has not been a male preserve for nearly ninety years. *Geoff Warnes*

Doncaster Corporation Transport Department did not convert a trolleybus route to motor-bus operation in one fell swoop. Instead, as new or reconditioned buses became available, they replaced one trolleybus at a time in the roster. So for some weeks before the final route, to Beckett Road, finally closed, only one trolleybus was running. This was 375, seen taking up its final load of fare-paying passengers at the stop in St Sepulchre Gate. The Christmas lights give a festive impression. As the previous picture makes obvious, a handful of other trolleys were still in the depot and could have been used had 375 failed, but this does not appear to have happened. So all the remaining photographs are of this one vehicle. The date is 14 December 1963.

David Packer

This last public journey provides a rare glimpse inside the lower saloon of 375. Space was fairly limited in buses of this vintage, which were narrower than modern vehicles. Incandescent bulbs provided the lighting, which was not as bright as this flash photograph makes it appear. Smoking was always forbidden downstairs, but was usually allowed on the top deck; of course, this had not mattered on open top trams! Special souvenir tickets were evidently available, with proceeds going to the Mayor's charity fund. *David Packer*

David Packer, whose photographs form the core of the trolleybus section of this book, has followed 375 to the end of the route on the circle at the top of Beckett Road. The conductor, Horace Bowers, and a couple of interested onlookers have a final word with the driver, Stanley Frith. Driving both motor and trolleybuses, as he was then doing, was not easy. The power pedal on the latter was on the left, so he remembers cornering very fast on occasions! And he was also tempted to overtake other trolleybuses, which couldn't be done. After the final run there was a dinner for all employees with forty years service and Stanley, who was three years short, was somewhat aggrieved to not be invited. *David Packer*

109

The final act of the drama, about half an hour later, was an official closing journey, for town councillors, the Mayor and long-serving transport employees. 375 gets ready to leave for the very last time from St Sepulchre Gate, which is seeing the end of electric urban transport after sixty-one years. When Huddersfield dispensed with its trolleybuses in 1968 one of them was illuminated with coloured lights for the final week, but Doncaster contented itself with a banner along the top deck reading '1928-1963 Doncaster's Last Trolleybus'. *David Packer*

And when all the public obsequies are done, there seems no one left in Greyfriars Road except for the crew and two schoolboys. Contrast this with the public enthusiasm for the launch of the electric trams in 1902. *Sic transit gloria mundi* makes an appropriate comment if rather an awful pun. But of course times had changed beyond recognition in over six decades. Back then, only the wealthy had any form of individual transport; by the 1960s, cars, motorbikes and scooters had given personal mobility to all classes. Trolleybuses, tied to what was even then a very limited part of Doncaster, must have seemed very parochial.
David Packer

As well as the nineteen bodies transferred to motor-buses, one complete trolleybus survived. 375 was donated by the Transport Department to the DO&LRS for preservation. Like many such vehicles, it had no obvious immediate home. It is pictured here in May 1965 at Stainforth in the yard of Premier, a former independent bus operator in the area. The yard is now part of a housing estate, but 375 was able to be moved in 1969 to the operational museum then established at Sandtoft in North Lincolnshire and has run again under the wires there. It is currently out of service awaiting repair and the DO&LRS would welcome donations towards the cost. *Howard Turner*

But there was still one surprise in store. On 8 August 1985 South Yorkshire PTE unveiled a modern trolleybus. Numbered 2450 in South Yorkshire Transport's fleet, the Dennis/Alexander bus was a standard front entrance vehicle, but powered by a GEC electric motor (diesel back-up allowed operation away from the wires too). 2450 ran experimentally along a one mile test track beside Doncaster Racecourse. The long-term aim was to reintroduce trolleybuses to both Doncaster and Rotherham, and legal powers were obtained for routes to Beckett and Lothian Roads, Intake and Wheatley Hills. However, bus deregulation meant that the plans had no chance of coming to fruition. 2450 is pictured here in 1986 on a visit to Sandtoft, where it remains today. *R Priestley*

Postscript

This book has studiously ignored the third transport mode operated by Doncaster Corporation, the motor bus. A brief glance at the competition offered to the trams and trolleybuses is however in order. Most of the early vehicles were built by the Bristol Company, and single-deckers of this type formed the bulk of the buses purchased in the period 1922-25. Two features which stand out are the solid tyres and the tremendously high steps which passengers had to negotiate to reach the saloon. No wonder the trolleybuses were more popular. *Charles Hall collection*

❖

The Transport Department eventually owned four of these Bristol A type double-deckers. The first were purchased in 1926 and originally had solid tyres, but this vehicle has been converted to run on pneumatics. The short body (not a pun on the body builders, Shorts of Belfast!) had four less seats than the contemporary six-wheel trolleybuses and passengers had to scale an external stairway at the rear. *Charles Hall collection*

Because of the absence of tram rails and the presence of trolleybus overhead, this picture of Hall Gate must date from later than the early 1930s. Traffic management is obviously already an issue, as the crossing is controlled by traffic lights and there is a 'No Waiting' sign on the pavement to the right.

The really intriguing thing is the bunting, flags and union jack shields festooning all the buildings and standards. Might it be a Royal visit to the Races? Or perhaps the Coronation of George VI in May 1937? If anyone knows, please tell us! *Charles Hall collection*

"THE TRAFFIC PROBLEM was solved expeditiously and well . . . . the new system of trolley buses,* following a circular route, proved to be remarkably efficient. The multitude no longer boarded what had come to be regarded as old fashioned tramcars. Those in Doncaster have all been abolished to make way for an extraordinarily efficient system of trolley buses which give greater mobility on the roads."

"Yorkshire Evening Post," Sept. 9th, 1931.

* A FLEET OF KARRIER SIX-WHEEL DOUBLE-DECKERS NUMBERING 26 VEHICLES

Karrier Motors produced this rather nice advertisement above in 1931 based on their construction of all but four of the then-existing Doncaster trolleybus fleet. Bus 11 and another vehicle are pictured working Race Day specials at the course. The press were obviously out in force, as were the punters, nearly all of them wearing the headgear then obligatory at all levels of society. Karriers did not even need to write their own copy, as the *Yorkshire Evening Post* had already done an excellent job for them. Three years later, when the first modern outline bus was produced, Karrier was again featuring Doncaster in its publicity.

Charles Hall collection

This is the same picture as that reproduced on page 71 above, but there is space here to show the busy street scene behind the trolleybus. There is already a considerable contrast to the days of the tram, with cars and motorbikes providing competition for both road space and passengers. Speedy, quiet and comfortable, transport by electric bus was definitely necessary if public transport was to retain its role.
Charles Hall collection

This trolleybus scaling the heights of Bradford towards the Clayton terminus is another South Yorkshire exile, though it is unrecognisable as the Mexborough & District single-decker it once was. The series of seven buses was purchased by Bradford in 1961 and were the last to enter service there, after rebodying by the East Lancashire company. The Clayton route closed in 1971, about eight months before the final run on 24 March 1972. The significance of that date is that it was the end of trolleybus operation in the United Kingdom as a whole, and despite the later South Yorkshire experiment, there has been no rebirth for the electric bus. *Michael Faulkner*

The opposite is true for the tram however, and South Yorkshire has been a leader in the introduction of modern light rail into the United Kingdom. On 23 May 1994, Her Royal Highness the Princess Anne formally opened the South Yorkshire Supertram system by unveiling a plaque at the centre of the tramway, on Park Square. The plaque is on the plinth to the left, the Princess is facing the camera in the centre of the picture, whilst behind her stands the Royal tram, number 12 in the twenty-five strong fleet of German-built trams. The extension of the tramway to Doncaster is rather unlikely however, although there are current plans to bring it into Rotherham. *The author*

TRAMWAY FLEET LIST

No.	Built	Scrap/Wdn	Type	Builder	Seats	Truck	Motors	Controllers	Notes
1-15	1902	1927/30	Open-top	ER&TCW	22/34	6′ Brill 21E	2x25hp DK25A	DK DB1 Form B	1, 2, 3
16-20	1903	1926/27/30	Open-top	ER&TCW	22/34	6′ Brill 21E	2x25hp DK25A	DK DB1 Form B	1, 2, 3
21-5	1903	1929/30	Open-top	ER&TCW	22/34	6′ Brill 21E	2x25hp DK25A	DK DB1 Form B	1, 4
26-31	1913	1927/31	Balcony	UEC	22/34	7′ 6″ P22	2x40hp DK20A	DK DB1 Form K3	
32	1913	1932	Balcony	UEC	32/42	13′ 6″ Radial	2x40hp DK20A	DK DB1 Form K3	5
33-6	1915-16	1931/33	Balcony	UEC	26/40	8′ 6″ P22	2x40hp DK20A	DK DB1 Form K3	6
37	1916	1925	Single	Mines Voss	20	5′ 6″ M&G40	2x27hp Westinghouse	Raworth	7
38-47	1920	1933/35	Vestibuled	EE	26/40	8′ 6″ P22	2x40hp DK30B	DK DB1 Form K3	
-	1902	c. 1925	Water Car	ER&TCW	-	6′ Brill 21E	2x25hp DK25A	DK DB1 Form B	
-	1903	c. 1935	Works Trailer	?	-	-	-	-	8

NOTES

1. Cars 1-25 were later equipped with BTH B18 controllers. 5-16 and 22-25 were equipped with top covers in four batches in 1907, 1909-10, 1910-11 and 1913. All were by UEC except for the third order, which was from Brush; cars 5-8 may well have been fitted with the latter. All cars converted had the original reversed stairs replaced by direct ones.

2. At least two cars had their truck cut and lengthened to 7′ on the Peckham P22 principle in 1913-15 (according to the Tramways Minutes, though some sources give 1921). 7 and 14 were definitely dealt with and 16 may also have been, perhaps in 1921, but the original intention to rebuild six cars was not carried out. A later proposal in 1925 to re-truck all top covered cars was not proceeded with.

3. 18/19/20 and possibly 3 rebuilt (in 1913?) with separate smoking and non-smoking compartments on the lower deck.

4. 23 and 24 were fitted with 7′ 6″ P22 trucks in 1922.

5. 32 had its Warner Patent radial truck (built by Peckham and of a design which rarely performed effectively) replaced by an 8′ 6″ Peckham P35 in 1925; this was purchased after a six month trial.

6. In May 1915 car 34 was reported as being involved in an accident, so at least some of this batch of new cars probably arrived in the earlier year; according to some sources, they all did.

7. Purchased from Erith Corporation Tramways in 1917 (their 15 or 16, the other had been sold to Dartford the previous year and destroyed by fire). According to one source, 37 was withdrawn as early as 1918, but in fact it was still having advertisements applied in December 1921 and was licensed the following January. Contrary to the intention of this one-man design, the car always ran with a conductor in Doncaster, thus making it uneconomic. 37 was scrapped in October 1925.

8. Former York horse car used as a salt and sand trailer; possibly purchased 1912.

9. Scrap/withdrawal dates are are taken from the records of the transport department and may refer to different stages of the process, ranging from the date of withdrawal, via the date it was decided to scrap a car, to the day on which the scrap dealer (usually a Mr Buxton) called to collect or (more usually) dismantle the car.

Builders & Equipment Suppliers for both Trams and Trolleybuses

Brill	J G Brill Co., Philadelphia, USA[1]
Bristol	Bristol Tranways & Carriage Co. Ltd.
Brush	Brush Electrical Engineering Co. Ltd., Loughborough
BTH	British Thomson-Houston Co. Ltd, Rugby
Bull	Bull Motors, Ipswich
BUT	British United Traction (a post-1946 amalgamation of the Leyland & AEC trolleybus interests)
Clough	Clough, Smith & Co Ltd, London[2]
DK	Dick, Kerr[3]
East Lancs	East Lancashire Coach Builders Blackburn
EE	English Electric[3]
ER&TCW	The Electric Railway & Tramway Carriage Works[3]
Garrett	Richard Garrett & Sons Ltd., Leiston, Suffolk
Karrier	Karrier Motors Ltd, Huddersfield (later Luton)
M&G	Mountain & Gibson Ltd, Bury
Metrovic	Metropolitan Vickers Co Ltd, Trafford Park (previously Westinghouse)
Milnes Voss	G C Milnes, Voss & Co, Birkenhead
Park Royal	Park Royal Vehicles Ltd, London
Peckham	Peckham Co, Kingston, NJ, USA[1]
Raworth	Raworth's Traction Patents Ltd.
Roe	Chas H Roe Ltd, Leeds
Sunbeam	Sunbeam Motors, Wolverhampton
UEC	United Electric Car Co.[3]

NOTES

1. Early tramcar trucks were usually of American design built under licence in the UK; Peckham trucks from the P22 onwards were built at their own British factory.

2. Suppliers and installers of trolleybus systems, not vehicle builders, but early Karriers were marketed jointly under the Clough name.

3. All refer to different departments of or stages in the evolution of the firm that became English Electric, based at Preston.

TROLLEYBUS FLEET LIST

No.	Registration No.	In Service	Disposal	Chassis Type	Body	Seats	Motors	Notes
1-4	DT 821/922/77/37	1928	1935-38	Garrett OS	Roe	28/32	Bull 65hp	1
5-10	DT 1099/118/43/6/93/1206	1928	1937-39	Karrier-Clough E6	Roe	28/32	BTH 60hp	2
11-16	DT 1745/6/7/9/8/50	1929	1939-45	Karrier-Clough E6	Roe	28/32	BTH 60hp	3
17-23	DT 2002/3/2165/6/7/8/2633	1930	1938-45	Karrier-Clough E6	Roe	28/32	BTH 60hp	3, 4
24-30	DT 3153-9	1931	1938-45	Karrier-Clough E6	Roe	28/32	BTH 60hp	3, 5
31	DT 2620	1932	1945	Bristol E	Beadle/Roe	27/33	BTH 60hp	6
(3)32	DT 4718	1934	1952	Karrier E6	Roe	28/32	BTH 60hp	7
(3)33-6	DT 5772-5	1935	1952-53	Karrier E6	Roe	28/32	Metrovic 80hp	
(3)37-42	DT 6539-44	1935-36	1952-54	Karrier E6	Roe	28/32	Metrovic 80hp	8
(3)43-8	ADT 181-6	1938	1955	Karrier E6	Roe	28/32	Metrovic 85hp	
(3)49-68	BDT 114-30/2-4	1939	1954-57	Karrier E6	Roe	28/32	Metrovic 80hp	9
(3)69-71	CDT 312-4	1943	1962-63	Karrier W	Park Royal Utility	26/30	Metrovic 85hp	10
(3)72-4	CDT 624-6	1945	1963	Karrier W	Brush Utility	26/30	Metrovic 85hp	11
(3)75-7	CDT 636-8	1945	1963	Karrier W	Park Royal Utility	26/30	Metrovic 85hp	12
378-83	LHN 780-85	1952	1959	BUT 9611T	East Lancs	26/30	EE120hp	13
384	BHJ 827	1954	1961	Sunbeam W	Brush Utility	26/30	BTH 85hp	14
385-92	BHJ 828/9/98-903	1954	1961-62	Sunbeam W	Park Royal Utility	26/30	BTH 85hp	15
393-8	EWT 478-80/513-15	1955	1962-63	Sunbeam W	Roe	28/34	Metrovic 85hp	16
351/2(2)	FNY 983/4	1957	1962	Karrier Sunbeam W	Roe	28/34	EE 85hp	17
353/4(2)	FWX 898/902	1958	1963	Sunbeam W	Roe	28/34	Metrovic 85hp	18

NOTES

1. 1 used for driver training duties only 03/04/28 - 20/08/28 and 01/06/36 - 31/07/38 The Bull motors may later have been replaced by standard BTH products. Registration numbers of 2-4 uncertain. The 3-axle chassis remained standard until 1939.

2. 6 withdrawn in 1937 following accident on North Bridge. 8 loaned in 1930 to Nottingham Corporation and to the Mexborough & Swinton Co. as a Karrier demonstrator. 10 had the first ever Karrier TB chassis.

NOTES (continued)

3. 12/14/15/20/23/25 stored at Leicester Avenue until December 1944 as possible replacements for war damaged vehicles.

4. 17 was Roe Commercial Co motor show exhibit at Olympia 1929. 20 (or perhaps 21) loaned to BBC for wireless interference tests 1930. 22 to Johannesburg 1/30 and York 04-5/01/31 (not 12/30, as in one source) as Karrier demonstrator and 23 supplied free in lieu of 22 in Jo'burg.

5. Last double-deckers where the top deck did not extend over the cab. The front destination boxes were built into the cab roof instead of into the windscreen. 29 was the last of the original design in service.

6. This was one of only two Bristol TBs ever built. The chassis was exhibited at the 1929 Commercial Motor Show and only afterwards bodied for Doncaster, probably with Beadle bodywork on a Roe frame. It came to Doncaster on extended trial on August 1930 and was purchased and numbered 31 on 11/02/32. The bus had a unique and over-effective electric brake. Seating may have been 28/31. N.B. The early history of this vehicle remains a matter of debate.

7. Chassis said to be chrome plated for the 1933 Commercial Motor Show. Many body details to Mr Potts' own design. The first 'flat fronted' body; all surviving buses from 32 onwards were renumbered into 3xx series in April 1948.

8. 37 was the Karrier/Roe exhibit in the 1935 Commercial Motor Show. 40-2 were the last to have smoking/non-smoking lower saloons and rear towing hooks.

9. 59 withdrawn after collision with 397. 62 loaned to Rotherham Corporation Transport for clearance tests prior to conversion to double-deck trolleybuses on 19/06/55. 65 withdrawn after collision with lorry. 68 was the last 3-axle bus.

10. The 2-axle utility W chassis was delivered under the name of both the then manufacturers, but could be designated to the operator's usual supplier. Doncaster opted for Karrier, but all the other second hand purchases were officially Sunbeams.. Unusually for a utility bus, 69 was delivered with upholstered seats instead of the usual wooden ones. All grey with one white band under the lower saloon windows till 1946, later withdrawn, chassis overhauled and given Roe bodies (seating 28/34) as ff: 369, 31/05/54 - 04/01/55; 370, 16/10/57 - 03/05/58; 371, 31/05/54 - 12/01/55; the Utility body on 70 had been re-pillared and re-panelled in 1952; the later new body was fitted to new Daimler bus 172 by Roe's in August 1962. 71 withdrawn after accident with Felix Motors bus and scrapped a little earlier than the others.

11. Roe bodies fitted as ff: 372, 05/07/54 - 24/01/55; 373, 05/07/54 - 31/12/54; 374, 31/12/54 - 18/02/55

12. All over chocolate livery until 1946. New Roe bodies fitted as ff: 375, 19/11/54 - 03/03/55; 376, 18/01/55 - 29/03/55; 377, 28/01/55 - 20/04/55. 375 had been re-pillared and re-panelled 1948, was the last trolley in service and has been preserved by Doncaster Omnibus & Light Railway Society at Sandtoft since 1969.

13. Ex-Darlington 68-73 (1949), also (like all wartime and post-war deliveries) 2-axle. Painted red with white window frames at first. 379/80 later in the three white band livery. All to one white band in 1956/7. All had emergency traction batteries till 1956. 81 was withdrawn early after an accident. All sold Bradford January 1960. 378 for spares, 379-83 rebodied with front entrance East Lancs bodies as 831-5. Withdrawn 1971. 834-5 at Sandtoft.

14. Ex-Southend on Sea 130 (1945). Withdrawn and rebodied with Roe 28/34 seat body, 29/09/58 - 03/03/59; body later fitted to new Daimler bus 169.

15. Ex-Southend on Sea 131-8 (1946). New Roe bodies, similar to 130's, fitted on dates below and later transferred to new Daimler chassis 184/68/85/7/6/3/2/73. 385, 25/04/58 - 01/12/58; 386, 28/11/58 - 01/05/59; 387, 13/08/56 - 29/03/57; 388, 18/09/56 - 25/03/57; 389, 25/02/56 - 02/08/57; 390, 12/03/57 - 02/08/57; 391, 23/02/58 - 01/09/58; 392, 30/05/58 - 11/12/58. 85 turned over in a collision with a coach at Spring Gardens/Cleveland Street 25/04/58. Withdrawn 31/12/61, but reinstated 01/02/62 due to a shortage following 371's scrapping after an accident.

16. Chassis with Brush B32C single deck bodies ex-Mexborough & Swinton Co. 1-6 (1943) acquired in November 1954. Overhauled by DCT and rebodied by Roe. All refitted to Leyland PD2/1 chassis, most being reconditioned, as ff: 94 (1947; preserved at Sandtoft), 189 (new), 188 (new, preserved by First Bus), 93(1947), 95 (1948) and 96 (1948).

17. Chassis ex-Pontypridd UDC 10-11 (1944). New bodies were fitted at Doncaster, later going to new Daimler buses 170-1. Both trolleys had automatic acceleration, but 351 had this removed and its EE motors replaced by Metrovic 85hp in 1960.

18. Chassis with Brush B32C single-deck bodies ex-Mexborough & Swinton Co. 14 and 18 (1947). New bodies went to 1951 Leyland PD2/1 124 and 123.

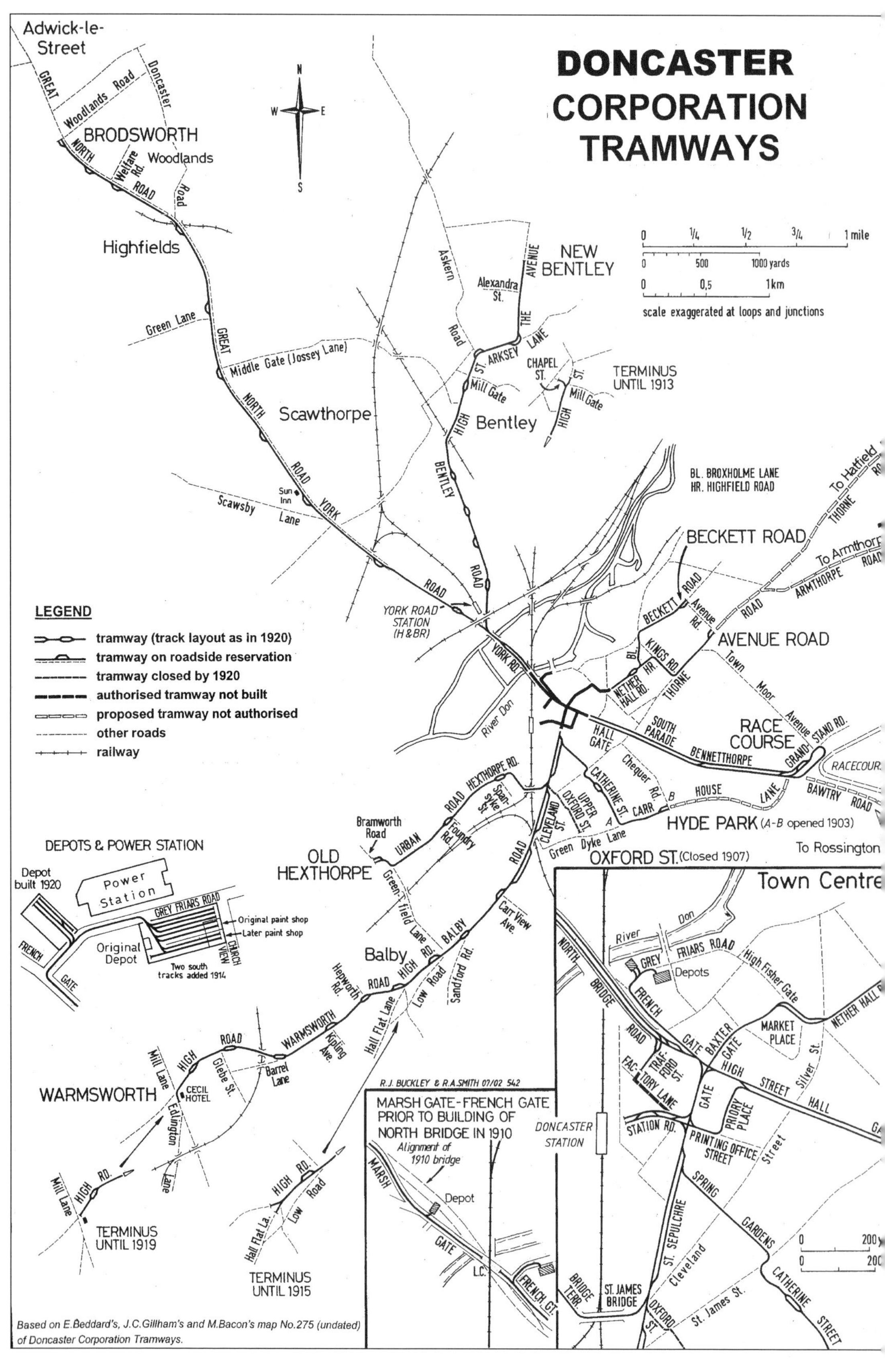

Based on E. Beddard's, J.C. Gillham's and M. Bacon's map No. 275 (undated) of Doncaster Corporation Tramways.

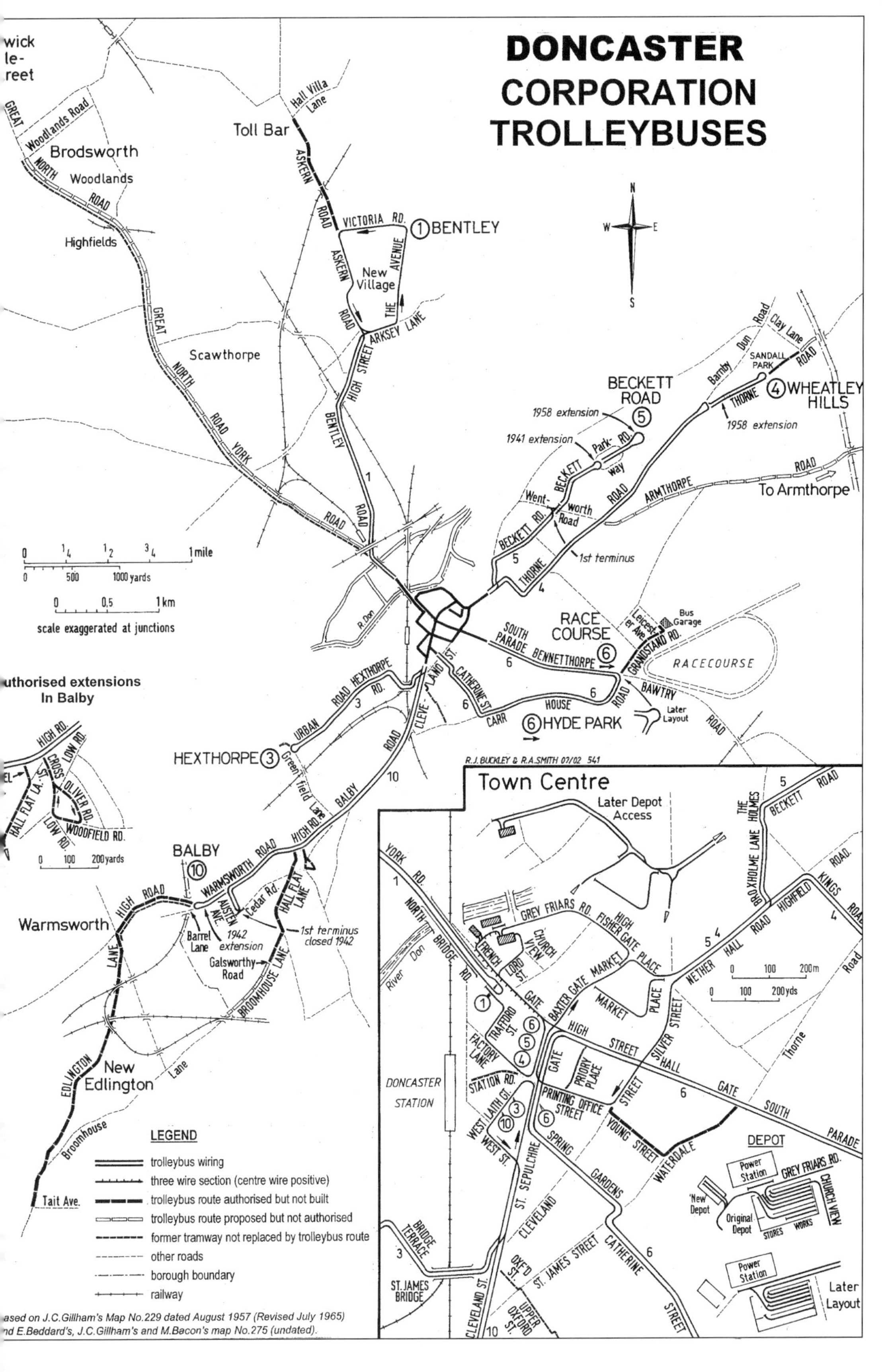

DONCASTER CORPORATION TROLLEYBUSES
N
W E
S
wick le-reet
Brodsworth
Woodlands
Highfields
GREAT NORTH ROAD
Woodlands Road
NORTH ROAD YORK ROAD
Scawthorpe
Hall Villa Lane
Toll Bar
ASKERN ROAD
VICTORIA RD.
BENTLEY 1
New Village
THE AVENUE
ARKSEY LANE
HIGH STREET
BENTLEY ROAD
Dun Road Clay Lane
Bamby
SANDALL PARK
THORNE ROAD
WHEATLEY HILLS 4
BECKETT ROAD 5
1958 extension
1941 extension
Park- way
Went- worth Road
BECKETT RD.
BECKETT ROAD
THORNE
1st terminus
1958 extension
ARMTHORPE ROAD
To Armthorpe
ROAD
1
5
4
R. Don
RACE COURSE
SOUTH PARADE
BENNETTHORPE
Leicester Ave.
Bus Garage
GRANDSTAND RD.
RACECOURSE
6
6
BAWTRY ROAD
Later Layout
CARR HOUSE
HYDE PARK 6
URBAN ROAD HEXTHORPE
HEXTHORPE 3
Green field Lane
CLEVELAND ST.
CATHERINE ST.
3 RD.
BALBY ROAD
10
authorised extensions In Balby
HIGH RD. LOW RD.
CROSS ST.
OLIVER RD.
HALL FLAT LA. ST.
LOW RD.
WOODFIELD RD.
0 100 200 yards
BALBY 10
WARMSWORTH ROAD
HIGH RD.
AUSTEN AVE.
Cedar Rd.
HALL FLAT LANE
1942 extension
1st terminus closed 1942
Barrel Lane
Galsworthy Road
BROOMHOUSE LANE
Warmsworth
HIGH ROAD LANE
EDLINGTON LANE
New Edlington
Broomhouse Lane
Tait Ave.
0 1/4 1/2 3/4 1 mile
0 500 1000 yards
0 0.5 1 km
scale exaggerated at junctions
R.J. BUCKLEY & R.A. SMITH 07/02 541
Town Centre
Later Depot Access
YORK RD.
NORTH BRIDGE RD.
River Don
FRENCH GATE
LORD ST.
Trafford ST.
FACTORY LANE
STATION RD.
DONCASTER STATION
WEST LAITH GT.
WEST ST.
Church View
GREY FRIARS RD.
HIGH FISHER GATE
BAXTER GATE MARKET
HIGH STREET
MARKET PLACE
CHURCH STREET
SILVER STREET
NETHER HALL ROAD
BROXHOLME LANE
THE HOLMES
BECKETT ROAD
HIGHFIELD ROAD
KINGS ROAD
Thorne ROAD
5
5
4
4
6
HALL GATE
PRIORY PLACE
PRINTING OFFICE STREET
YOUNG STREET
WATERDALE
SOUTH PARADE
SPRING GARDENS
CLEVELAND ST.
ST. SEPULCHRE
ST. JAMES STREET
CATHERINE STREET
OXF'D
UPPER OXFORD ST.
CLEVELAND ST.
BRIDGE TERRACE
ST. JAMES BRIDGE
DEPOT
Power Station
GREY FRIARS RD.
CHURCH VIEW
'New Depot
Original Depot
STORES WORKS
Power Station
Later Layout
0 100 200 m
0 100 200 yds
LEGEND
trolleybus wiring
three wire section (centre wire positive)
trolleybus route authorised but not built
trolleybus route proposed but not authorised
former tramway not replaced by trolleybus route
other roads
borough boundary
railway
ased on J.C.Gillham's Map No.229 dated August 1957 (Revised July 1965)
nd E.Beddard's, J.C.Gillham's and M.Bacon's map No.275 (undated).

Bearing out what was said above about growing road traffic between the wars, this pre-1914 scene shows the single tram line in High Street leading up from Clock Corner. In the absence of a tram, there is no mechanical transport on the road at all, just crowds of pedestrians and a single horse and trap. *Author's collection*

126

The name plate of Hadfield's Foundry, Sheffield, on a centre-groove tramway point. This one was actually manufactured for Hull, but it could well have been part of a joint order for Doncaster, which also used the firm's products. *The author*